Journey to
HEALING
& Cherry Popsicles Too

Jeremiah 29:11

[signature]

Kyle Duvall

xulon PRESS

Copyright © 2015 by Kyle Duvall

Journey to Healing & Cherry Popsicles Too
by Kyle Duvall

Printed in the United States of America.

ISBN 9781498457644
Edited by Xulon Press.

All rights reserved solely by the author. The author guarantees all contents are original and do not infringe upon the legal rights of any other person or work. No part of this book may be reproduced in any form without the permission of the author. The views expressed in this book are not necessarily those of the publisher.

Unless otherwise indicated, Scripture quotations taken from the English Standard Version (ESV). Copyright © 2001 by Crossway, a publishing ministry of Good News Publishers. Used by permission. All rights reserved.

Scripture quotations taken from the Holman Christian Standard Bible (HCSB). Copyright © 1999, 2000, 2002, 2003, 2009 by Holman Bible Publishers. Used by permission. All rights reserved.

Scripture quotations taken from the King James Version (KJV) – public domain

Scripture quotations taken from the New International Version (NIV). Copyright © 1973, 1978, 1984, 2011 by Biblica, Inc.™. Used by permission. All rights reserved.

Scripture quotations taken from the New International Version (NIV). Copyright © 1973, 1978, 1984, 2011 by Biblica, Inc.™. Used by permission. All rights reserved.

www.xulonpress.com

Is it possible to find joy in something as simple as a cherry Popsicle? Is it possible to awaken every morning with an attitude of thanksgiving when the night was spent in agonizing pain? Is it possible to choose to walk toward life even in the midst of heartbreaking grief? Kyle Duvall not only believes it; he lives it and shows us how.

Kyle takes his readers on his personal journey through illness and grief and gives an honest and poignant look at our mortality. In a very heartwarming fashion, he demonstrates how daily gratitude, intentional expressions of thanksgiving, and quiet meditation are tools anyone can use to maintain stability in difficult times. If you are struggling with the challenges of life, this book will encourage and inspire you to choose to walk toward life.

Ken Corr, D.Min
Congregational Care Minister
Brentwood Baptist Church, Brentwood, TN

"Into every life, a little rain must fall." However, some people seem to get more than their fair share. As fate would have it, I have had the privilege to be on the sidelines of Kyle's life. I personally observed how he gracefully managed the storms that seemed to come, one after another, like the waves of the ocean. There were moments when events swamped him, and he was left gasping for air, both literally and figuratively ... it was obvious that he clung even more tightly to his abiding faith like a life preserver as the storms of life washed over him.

While reading *Journey to Healing & Cherry Popsicles Too,* I relived those moments I witnessed when Kyle endured the latest troubles that threatened to test him to the breaking point. In my mind's eye, I can still see the determination and strength he would draw on as he quoted one of his favorite scriptures: *"This is the day the Lord has made. I will rejoice and be glad in it."* The pain would not necessarily go away, but there was an abiding peace that steadied him and an assurance that grace would see him through.

If you are experiencing more than your fair share of rain, within the pages of this book, you can find battle-tested nuggets of truth to see you through your storm.

Daryl R. Murray
Founder/Executive Director
Welcome Home Ministries, Nashville, TN

Romans 5 boldly declares that in our afflictions we can not only endure but also rejoice, because in the midst of our struggle, God is producing in us a *"hope that will not disappoint."*

In *Journey to Healing & Cherry Popsicles Too*, my friend, Kyle Duvall, is a living testimony to this hope. Kyle vividly takes on the journey through the ups and downs of life and yet demonstrates how God's goodness and mercy can be found each step of the way.

Kyle is one of the most passionate people I know, and in his story you will find echoes of your own, including valuable insights into the *"grace in which we stand"* when life tries to knock us down.

Jay Strother
Campus and Teaching Pastor
The Church at Station Hill, Spring Hill, TN

Kyle Duvall reminds readers about valuable "Lessons in Living" that are consistent with God's Word: Count your blessings, and thank Jesus for each one. Remember, every breath and every heartbeat is a gift from God.

What if you awaken tomorrow and *all* the blessings that you failed to thank the Lord for today are gone? You have the greatest possession in the world—the Lord.

I commend and congratulate Kyle for his story about God's wisdom. The Lord has something to teach each of us in every circumstance and situation. Always ask, what is good about this? The Lord will show the answer. Also, each person has a story about what Jesus has done in his or her life. Share it with others so the Lord can bless them.

As you read about Kyle's life-changing story, allow the Lord to speak directly to you. He spoke to me.

Ralph E. Vaughn
President
Tennessee Christian Chamber of Commerce

Kyle, in his near-death experience, makes a conscious decision to "walk toward life." He just doesn't think about it, but makes small, painful steps toward recovery. This inspiring book encourages us to keep moving forward in spite of the hardships and embrace life.

Chris Yates
Host of CCM Classic, Nationally Syndicated Radio Show
Senior Marketing Consultant/Event Producer
94FM The Fish, Nashville, TN

To my dear wife
— Emily Sue Duvall —
Emily is the love of my life; she has bravely and faithfully journeyed with me during the tumultuous storms of my life. Her tender touch and loving presence have strengthened me and helped me survive when sickness threatened my very existence. To Kyle David Duvall Jr., whose battle with cancer since childhood has helped me face my own mortality with renewed faith and hope that God will wipe away every tear in heaven's kingdom, where there is no more sorrow, sickness, or suffering. Last, but not least, to my daughter, Keli Sue Duvall Lawrence, who has demonstrated beauty and grace

since the difficult days of her childhood, as she endured the many years of her brother's struggle to survive cancer. Her radiant love continues to shine as a beacon of hope and a bulwark of strength for our family.

To God Be All the Glory!

For My Triplet Grandbabies
"The Trips" + Two!

Ava Arielle Duvall
Austin Kyle Duvall
Autumn Belle Duvall
&
Tristan Dean Lawrence
Macy Emma Lawrence

TABLE OF CONTENTS

Introduction xv

Chapter 1 This Was *My* Vacation! Oh, Boy! . . . 23
Chapter 2 Awakening to Your Pain
　　　　　with a Grateful Heart 29
Chapter 3 Find a Reason for Hope 37
Chapter 4 It's Gonna Take a While to Heal . . . 45
Chapter 5 Gratitude 53
Chapter 6 Thanksgiving Day. 59
Chapter 7 Running a Marathon 65
Chapter 8 Limited LifeTIME Warranty—
　　　　　Uncertainty and Blessings 77
Chapter 9 Flashback. 89
Chapter 10 Healing of the Soul 99
Chapter 11 Tragedy 107
Chapter 12 Barrett's Funeral 115
Chapter 13 Losing Mom 119
Chapter 14 Experiencing Grief 129
Chapter 15 The Glare of Death 137
Chapter 16 God's Merciful Grace 141
Parting Words. 149

Introduction

For I will restore health to you, and your wounds I will heal, declares the Lord. (Jeremiah 30:17 ESV)

Several days after the emergency surgery that saved my life, I awoke in the intensive care unit of the hospital. I was lying flat on my back in excruciating pain. I didn't know where I was, or why I was hooked up to so many intravenous devices, which were attached to both my arms and my neck. A heart monitor was flashing, and as consciousness more fully returned with intensifying pain, I began to take a body survey, hoping all my body parts were still intact and nothing was missing!

My entire abdomen was covered with a surgical dressing. Two drainage tubes protruded from both sides of my abdomen, and a third very large drainage/bypass tube was implanted into my stomach at the top of my abdomen near my heart.

My lips were parched. I pleaded with the nurse for a drink of water to quench my thirst.

The nurse responded, "I am so sorry, but you can't have water."

I groaned, "But I'm thirsty."

The nurse stood over me with compassion and offered me what he could—a tiny spongelike swab that was dipped in water. He gently touched my lips with the swab, allowing me to suck a few droplets of water from it to soften my parched lips. He used an additional wet swab to wipe the inside of my mouth, under my tongue and on the surface of my gums to help relieve the aridity.

My body was in shambles—ravaged—a far cry from my athletic tone due to an intense workout regiment, which only days before had consisted of one hundred push-ups, one hundred sit-ups, weight lifting, and elliptical cardiovascular training that rivaled even the most fit of athletes half my age. My body was in a desperate state of affairs.

When I made my first efforts at moving, the pain was unbearable. Turning from side to side in the hospital bed was out of the question; that was not happening. And as I gazed at my body with all the devices hooked to it to save and sustain my life, I literally felt like a puppet attached to many strings.

I remained motionless on my back, except for moving my head from side to side, or when I reached up through the wires and other body attachments to push the nurse "call button."

Oh, how desperate I was for living water to quench my thirst, renew my spirit, and make me whole again.

For the next week, my diet consisted of eating ice chips. This was a treat, given that immediately after surgery I was only allowed to suck on a tiny dampened swab to relieve the desert dryness in my mouth.

Eventually, I was allowed to have something to eat other than ice chips. The first thing I ate was a Blue Bell Cherry Popsicle (clear liquid diet only). At that very moment, that cherry Popsicle was by far the best tasting food on the planet. There was no cuisine in any five-star restaurant that could have rivaled or matched the wondrous taste of that Blue Bell Cherry Popsicle. Really? Yes! It is not up for debate. Besides, I'm telling the story.

How grateful I was for the first taste of that wonderfully cool, moist, and flavorful Blue Bell Cherry Popsicle. More important, that Popsicle became symbolic to me of the small, but very important and necessary steps I must take during my journey to healing and wholeness.

You may smile, but there is so much of life we take for granted. Yet, it was something as simple and as gloriously tasty as a cherry Popsicle that stirred gratitude within my spirit for the simple things of life that gave me hope and pointed me in the direction of healing and wholeness.

You may struggle with cancer or some other dreadful disease, an addiction, the loss of a loved one, or some terrible circumstance in your life that threatens your well-being, physically, emotionally, or spiritually. There is hope, even though your journey toward healing and wholeness may have many hurdles to overcome. You can do it with God's help, but there is much "homework" you will have to do to achieve wholeness.

So, as we begin our journey together toward healing and wholeness, let's begin with a few very important steps:

Step One: **Have a positive attitude focused on directness of purpose and a resolve rooted in gratitude for life**. Resist the temptation to give in to the distraction of your pain, which you know is there, and perhaps is constant, during your recovery (physically, emotionally, and/or spiritually).

Introduction

***Step Two:* Recognize the little things in your life that encourage hope during the process of your healing and recovery**—like a Blue Bell Cherry Popsicle. Try to recognize even the smallest kernel of hope in the midst of your pain. What is *your* symbolic Blue Bell Cherry Popsicle that encourages hope?

***Step Three:* Offer a prayer of gratitude and thanksgiving for the rays of hope you discover during the journey along the path of your healing.** Have an attitude of gratitude. Yes, it rhymes. Say it several times to yourself: *An attitude of gratitude ... an attitude of gratitude ... an attitude of gratitude!* Got it? Pray that God will help you have an attitude of gratitude, regardless of your circumstances, so that you may recognize the nuggets of hope along the way, during your process of healing.

Why is gratitude so important to our healing? It is gratitude that steers our minds away from our pain and/or a smoldering obsession with our terrible circumstances to focus on the goodness of life and living.

Offer upward a prayer of gratitude for life—for the fact that you are alive at this moment during your struggle. Believe me, the pain you are feeling is overwhelming evidence that you are, indeed, alive. I feel very much alive in the midst of my pain and healing—at this very moment.

"Thank you, God, for the pain of healing." It's a paradoxical prayer but one you can pray with gratitude in your heart for life, no matter your circumstances.

Finally, have you discovered your nugget or ray of hope—your "Blue Bell Cherry Popsicle?" Name it, and contemplate the thought of its simplicity for a moment. Have you offered a prayer of gratitude for the goodness of life and living in the midst of your difficult circumstances?

Pause right now, and do this exercise: *Contemplate a symbol for your hope, and offer gratitude and thanksgiving to God for the goodness of life and living.* Now, let's journey together toward healing and wholeness throughout these pages.

Parenthetically, I began writing this book, including portions of the introduction, as I was recuperating at home within weeks of leaving the hospital. I still had medical paraphernalia attached to my body, particularly a terrible stomach bypass tube, which remained in place until my stomach regenerated enough to have the tube surgically removed. I was experiencing *much pain* and a slow process of healing as I began to write.

Introduction

Nevertheless, I decided to take my time writing this book over a period of two years to reflect on the process of healing in my life, even though I had no idea that tragedy and trying times would shake me to the core of my being during those next two years. Yet even during the most painful moments, my gratitude for life with the "nuggets of hope" I discovered along the way encouraged me toward healing and wholeness; and through it all, I have found so much joy and gratitude for the life God continues to breathe into my soul at the dawning of each new day I live.

My prayer for you as you journey with me through the pages of this book is that you will find encouragement, hope, healing, and wholeness in your life, because at some point in all our lives, no matter who we are, we all need healing in some dynamic way.

Chapter 1

This Was My Vacation! Oh, Boy!

It was the first day of my vacation. My wife Emily, my sister Tammy, and her good friend Rosanna, and I were traveling from Spring Hill, Tennessee, a suburb of Nashville, to Gulf Shores, Alabama. I was so ready to enjoy a week of much-needed rest, relaxation, and recreation.

Emily has a friend, Susan Rodgers, who owns a three-bedroom resort condominium in Gulf Shores, and we were on our way to the resort condo to enjoy some fun in the sun on the beach.

We arrived in Gulf Shores in the late afternoon and decided to eat dinner at Throw Rolls, an incredibly popular restaurant with some great down-home country cookin'. And, yes, the waiters and waitresses throw rolls to you (or at you) from across the room. All you have to do is get their attention by waving at them, like the catcher at home plate signaling the pitcher on the mound. Go ahead! Throw a fastball or a curveball! Of course, some of us have better hand-eye coordination than others, which explains why the rolls smacked Emily right in her face. It's really great food, even though most of the "throw rolls" landed in our laps rather than on our plates.

This was the beginning of a great vacation! This was *my* vacation. Oh, boy!

Although the atmosphere was delightfully fun, I wasn't feeling very well. I was a bit nauseated, so I decided to eat in moderation and enjoyed mostly vegetables, along with the table conversation. Rosanna just had to do the tourist thing by taking photos with her iPhone to send back to her husband so he could experience the fun Rosanna was enjoying and he was missing—rub it in, rub it in. "Come on, Rosanna, that's your fourth photo of a plate full of food!" Flash, Flash, Flash! "Enough, already!" But we were having fun!

After dinner, we returned to the condo for the evening. I became more nauseated, and my stomach was getting tighter than a tick's belly; my belly felt like it was going to pop! I rested in bed

This Was My Vacation! Oh, Boy!

for about an hour. The nausea worsened, until I began to heave with uncontrollable vomiting.

Five years earlier, I had suffered a blockage caused by a kink in my small intestines that required emergency surgery. It was terrible surgery that landed me in the hospital for ten days. Surely, I was not experiencing the same problem again.

Emily and Tammy helped me to the car to make an emergency run to the nearest hospital. We were a long way from home, approximately 450 miles, and had no idea where the nearest medical facility was.

Emily wheeled into a twenty-four-hour emergency care clinic near our condo with the hope the clinical staff could offer some immediate care, but we were quickly sent on our way because the clinical staff could not provide the care the attending physician thought I needed. We were told we must get to the South Baldwin Medical Center in Foley, Alabama, as soon as possible.

"Foley? What? Where is Foley?"

Phone calls were made en route for directions to the hospital, but we got lost along the way.

"Please, God, help us find the hospital!"

I felt every jiggle and bump in the road, as my heaving and vomiting increased. My stomach was looking more and more like I was with child, and my heaving rivaled even the most severe morning sickness women experience during pregnancy. But I wasn't pregnant. Oh, how I wished I were!

Yeah, I know, I am a guy, and you think "man pregnancy" is impossible. But when you are in the throws of vomiting, it is very easy to wish for the impossible; and at that moment, I wished for pregnancy, so I could push this thing that had invaded my stomach out of my body before my stomach exploded!

The small trash can I was holding between my legs in the front passenger's seat of the car became my consoling best friend as Emily continued to find every bump and pothole in the road, as she desperately searched for the hospital in a town named Foley. Indeed, it was a very dark night.

"Oh, there's a nice big pothole. Let's see if we can drive through the middle of it. WAIT! Is that a deer up ahead caught in our headlights?"

This was my vacation? Oh, boy! Really?

Mercifully, after an ordeal that took more than an hour, Emily finally found the South Baldwin Medical Center through the help and navigation of the hospital staff on the other end of her cell phone.

I was in serious trouble, lying propped up on the gurney in the emergency room. I could not recline onto my back without suffering excruciating pain,

This Was My Vacation! Oh, Boy!

because of the increasing pressure on my stomach. An hour turned into two hours. The emergency room staff attended to my care as best they could, but they were not aware of how seriously ill I was, until the CT scanner was available to assist a diagnosis. It was late on a Saturday evening, and the small town emergency room was overwhelmed with people who needed attention.

A tube was inserted into my nose, down my throat and into my stomach to pump out the excess fluid in my stomach in hopes of relieving the mounting pressure, but very little fluid was relieved. This was not a good sign! It suggested that I had a more severe problem.

Emily stood beside the gurney in the emergency room cradling my head in her hands and holding it close to her chest. Just before I lost consciousness, I feared I might die. I faintly pleaded with Emily, "Please don't let me die in this emergency room. I need help now."

Later, I discovered that Emily had held my head and trembling body for hours.

Once the surgeon arrived, he immediately read the CT scan and prepped for surgery. The CT scan was alarming! The surgeon's hope that I would survive the surgery was diminishing as I was wheeled into surgery. He told Emily that if I had family members nearby that she should call them to the hospital, that my heart was in atrial fibrillation and I had multiple organ problems and failure.

Emily sat alone in a surgical waiting room 450 miles from home, as she waited for a positive word from the surgeon. There were no family members or church members sitting with her to comfort her growing concerns.

A kind nurse brought her a blanket at dawn. She called family members and dear friends throughout the night and early morning hours to ask for prayers. She prayed for me until 2:30 PM, the following day, after a harrowing evening of a life-threatening emergency. Then, after six hours of surgery and an additional two and a half hours in the recovery room to stabilize my vital signs, Emily was allowed to see me in the intensive care unit of the hospital. Tammy and Rosanna returned to the hospital, where they stayed with Emily. They sat together, watched, waited, and prayed. This was *my* vacation! Oh, boy!

Chapter 2

Awakening to Your Pain with a Grateful Heart

I will never leave you or forsake you.
(Hebrews 13:5 HCSB)

When I awoke after surgery, I was in the intensive care unit. I don't recall the first couple of days in ICU. The nurse told me that was a blessing, since I had a tube in my right nostril, which extended to my stomach to relieve stomach pressure, and another tube in my left nostril that helped me breathe, along with an oxygen mask. I was told that at one point there were nineteen tubes, intravenous lines, and/or monitor electrodes attached to my body.

Additionally, while in the ICU, my breathing began to slow, so much so that my body struggled for breath—literally, the breath of life. This caused my body to convulse. The convulsions were so violent that my wrists were strapped to the bedsides to restrain my arms. A nurse had to sit beside my bed for an entire shift to monitor my breathing and shake me to stimulate my breathing, when my breath became shallow. I have no recollection of this experience, which as the nurse told me, was, indeed, a blessing. Yet as painful as it was when I awoke to awareness from surgery, I was alive! I was grateful I had awakened to live for another day!

You may have cancer, or you may have struggled with a disease for months, even years. An accident or illness may have suddenly assaulted you, requiring immediate, life-saving emergency surgery. Perhaps the struggle bearing down on you is a broken heart, due to a failed relationship or an addiction that has held you in bondage for many years. Whatever your circumstance, once you awaken to your pain, you will have a choice to make, even in excruciating pain—physically, emotionally, or spiritually. You can choose to thank God for the life you have in this present moment, no matter your circumstances or how faint you may feel, or you can choose to wallow in your pain and self-pity, which is self-defeating and a great inhibitor to healing.

Don't get me wrong. I am not talking about ignoring your pain. Just don't give into it, and especially the negative thoughts that often accompany pain.

My physical pain was excruciating when I awoke from surgery, and you can bet I relied on the hospital staff and pain management experts to assist me to better tolerate my pain. It also helped me to have a loved one by my side who intervened for me at the nurse's station when my call button was not answered in a timely manner. Keep in mind there are many patients in a hospital and they can overwhelm the nursing staff, which is why it is good to have a loved one assist you as your advocate.

Regardless of whether your pain is physical, spiritual, or emotional (I experienced all three simultaneously), a loved one can provide much support and comfort. I recall Emily simply sitting at my beside, holding my hand and praying for me when I struggled so desperately. Her presence and prayers were the two most important things I needed in my darkest moments. Sometimes, there are no words to utter in prayer but just a simple touch with moments of prayerful silence.

While there are some challenging physical and emotional realities that cannot be ignored, there is much we can do spiritually to calm our spirit, even when our body is in shambles. This also applies when recovering from the trauma of an extended illness or even a tragedy of life's circumstances—the loss of a job, a divorce, or the loss of a loved one.

Push the "call button" metaphorically. Get help from a qualified counselor or your pastor. Lean on your dearest friends, who continue to love you in the "ups and downs" of your life; but don't wallow in the trauma of your circumstances or self-pity. When you need help, push the call button. Push whatever buttons are necessary to receive the help you need to assist in your journey toward healing, health, and wholeness.

It is easy to give into feelings of abandonment, or to feel scared and alone when we are hurting physically, emotionally, or spiritually. Intentionally direct your mind to Scriptures that are most comforting to you during these moments of fear and anxiety in order to focus your mind beyond your pain and to help calm your spirit.

O, how I prayed, and as I did, a fragment of a Bible verse, like a still small voice, quietly and gently comforted my spirit: *"I will never leave you or forsake you"* (Hebrews 12:5 HCSB).

Awakening to Your Pain with a Grateful Heart

Christ's presence is with you no matter your circumstances. Wrap yourself in it, and don't let the negative voices that accompany your circumstances rob you of God's abiding presence.

I recall the emotion I felt as Hebrews 12:5 penetrated my heart; it was a healing salve. I was so afraid I was not going to make it. It was a fear like I had never experienced in my life. Yet Christ's promise to me as His child—that He would not leave me or forsake me—helped calm my spirit and ease my emotional and spiritual pain.

So many times I have heard the expression, "I don't know what the future holds, but I know who holds the future." If ever there is a time to cling to hope with a grateful heart, it is at the very moment we embrace the reality that *nothing* can separate us from the love of God in Christ Jesus—in the present moment or the unforeseen future!

For I am convinced that neither death, nor life, neither angels nor demons, neither the present nor the future, nor any powers, neither height nor depth, nor anything else in creation, will be able to separate us from the love of God that is in Christ Jesus our Lord. (Romans 8:38-39 NIV)

In my desperate circumstances, I embraced the fact that I am a child of God. Then, I began to recite the Twenty-third Psalm, while visualizing

God's love and mercy as a wonderful oasis of hope and grace:

The Lord is my shepherd; I shall not want. He maketh me to lie down in green pastures: he leadeth me beside the still waters. He restoreth my soul: he leadeth me in the paths of righteousness for his name's sake. Yea, though I walk through the valley of the shadow of death, I will fear no evil: for thou art with me; thy rod and thy staff they comfort me. Thou preparest a table before me in the presence of mine enemies: thou anointest my head with oil; my cup runneth over. Surely goodness and mercy shall follow me all the days of my life: and I will dwell in the house of the Lord forever. (Psalm 23 KJV)

I visualized grazing in a field of green grass as a lamb under the watchful care of my Shepherd. I felt the breeze on my face as I lay in those green pastures. I gazed at the pond of glassy water that was still—very still; it was a perfect calm. This brought much serenity to my spirit and restored my soul, even though I was physically weak, wounded, and shaken from the experience of walking through "the valley of the shadow of death." Yet, Christ's voice kept reassuring me, as he said over and over to me, "Fear not. No evil will overtake you, because I am with you. My rod and staff will not only guide you to health and wholeness but will also protect you from all harm." Then, Jesus invited me to partake of the food of His loving grace, even while threats to my life were still present. He said to me, "Kyle, my grace is sufficient for your needs" (See 2 Corinthians 12:8-10). He touched my head, my heart, and my body with the warmth of His compassion and grace. He quenched my parched, dry lips with a cup that overflowed with water.

As I began to drift off to sleep, I heard God's reassuring voice deep within my spirit say to me, "You are my child. I am with you today, tomorrow, and throughout all eternity."

Meditation

Take a few moments to read Psalm 23 and visualize the Shepherd taking care of you in the midst of your painful circumstances. Once you finish this visualization, close your eyes; and with an attitude of gratitude, offer a prayer of thanksgiving in your heart to God for the breath you breathe at this moment that sustains your life. Continue in the stillness and serenity in focused prayer. Offer gratitude to God for the Shepherd's presence, which will abide with you throughout eternity. Now rest in the comforting presence of the Lord.

Chapter 3

Find A Reason For Hope

*This is the day the Lord has made;
let us rejoice and be glad in it. (Psalm
118:24 HCSB)*

Once I could actually get out of bed, two physical therapists were there to encourage me to take a few steps with the assistance of a walker. The physical therapists managed the IV pole, while making sure I was steady enough to walk. As I exited my room, one of the therapists asked me, "Which direction do you want to go?"

Even at that moment those words became a metaphor to me, far beyond the meaning of the intended question posed by the physical therapist. It was one of the little nuggets of hope that inspired me to choose a direction toward healing and wholeness. You see, I was alive and grateful.

To the right was a long hallway leading to a picture window at the end of a corridor. To the left was a shorter hallway that led to a chapel. I asked the physical therapists, "What's down the hallway, beyond the chapel?" One of the therapists said, "Well, there's a corridor that leads to a neo-natal nursery."

I made my choice. I told the therapists, "I want to walk toward life. I want to experience birth, the beginning of new life." The therapists smiled. They got it. Did you get it?

Are you walking toward healing and wholeness? Are you walking toward life? I couldn't walk on my own without assistance during those early days of recovery. My steps were slow, but I was shuffling toward life with every small and methodical step I took.

Your circumstances may have crippled your spirit, but as painful as your circumstances seem, when you awoke this morning, it was the dawning of a new day.

You stand at the crossroads of your journey toward healing and wholeness. You have a choice to make. Will you choose to make this day a new beginning and begin it with an attitude of gratitude? Choose this day to walk toward life, even if you stumble through the day.

The physical therapists supported me as I slowly made my first efforts at walking down the hallway toward the neonatal nursery. As I reached the chapel, I asked the physical therapists if I could stop to offer a prayer of gratitude for life. I was alive and breathing in that present moment. My spirit was overflowing with gratitude.

As I entered the chapel, I noticed a small altar with a cross and a large altar Bible. I held tightly to my walker but slowly turned the pages of the Bible to one of my favorite Psalms, which contains my prayer of thanksgiving for life: *"This is the day the Lord has made; let us rejoice and be glad in it"* (Psalm 118:24 HCSB).

Tears welled up in my eyes, not simply from the physical pain I was experiencing, but also because this is the verse I quote every morning when I awake and look out my bedroom window to greet the new day—in sickness or in health. This, indeed, was the day the Lord had made, and I was alive in it and grateful for it!

I continued with the assistance of the physical therapists to walk beyond the chapel to the baby nursery down the corridor.

One of the physical therapists said, "It's been two weeks since I've seen a baby in those cribs. They're usually with their mothers."

This didn't matter to me. What mattered was I was walking toward life! My direction was set! My hope and resolve were focused on beholding the newness of life, even though I was broken, bent, and barely shuffling my feet, literally with every baby step I took.

As I grew a bit stronger with the help of nurses, family members, and the frequent visits of physical therapists in the days to come, I made the ritualistic walk toward life—the chapel, the Bible on the altar, and that neonatal nursery—everyday.

Then, it happened! After a week of hoping to see a newborn baby in the hospital nursery, there it was as I rounded the corner: newborn life! I could hardly wait to press my nose against the nursery window to gaze and welcome a newborn baby boy to planet earth. He was only minutes old.

I thought to myself, "What a large baby! He was born a toddler! His poor mother!"

Then, I smiled, as I thought of my triplet grandbabies born to my son and daughter-in-law just a few months earlier: Ava Arielle, Austin Kyle, and Autumn Belle. I recalled saying to my son, "Do you realize that if you combined the length of the triplets at birth that your wife had four feet of babies inside her (16 inches + 16 inches + 15½ inches)?" Oh, Mama!

Then, two months after the birth of the triplets, my darling daughter and son-in-law put the cherry on top of the three-layered cake, when Keli gave birth to a beautiful baby boy, Tristan Dean Lawrence, who was exactly one-month-old on the day of my near-death sickness and life-changing emergency surgery.

I couldn't help but reflect on how much I missed—and wanted to see—my four grandbabies, as I gazed at the precious newborn baby boy in the hospital nursery. I was 450 miles from home. I had a very long way to travel, literally and figuratively, before I would make it back home. Yet I had four grand-reasons to keep shuffling my way toward newborn life. This birthing moment was another one of those golden nuggets (another Blue Bell Cherry Popsicle) along the path of my journey that encouraged me to push myself toward healing, health, and wholeness.

As I continued to focus my attention on every movement of that little (gigantic) baby boy in the hospital nursery, I noticed how innocently naked and vulnerable he was. It dawned on me how vulnerable I was; and judging from the gap in the back of my hospital gown, I was looking pretty naked too! I know, I was sick, but even as poorly as I felt, I didn't want to look crazy. Sick people don't want to look sick *and crazy!* Go ahead and laugh. But try closing the gap in those dreadful hospital gowns with intravenous paraphernalia and three abdominal tubes protruding from your body!

I did what I could to cover my naked innocence, but I was still left with my vulnerability. Like the baby in the hospital nursery who needed much attention and care to survive, the shuffling baby steps I took indicated to me that it would take a very long time for me to grow into the strength, health, and wholeness that I so desperately desired.

Before turning to leave that blessed moment of experiencing the newness of life, I smiled as I watched that little baby boy exercise his lungs. He breathed in and out a cry for attention and care. Oh, how my soul cried out to God for His help. Yet, as the tears began to flow down my face, they turned into tears of great joy and gratitude for sustaining life.

Once, again, I thanked God for new life that both the newborn baby and I shared in common at that very moment. It was the dawning, the birth, of a new day. God had breathed into both of us

His breath of life, and in our own way, with vastly different circumstances, we became living souls.

Meditation

As difficult as it is for you during the intensity of your struggles, offer praise to God in prayer. Memorize the following scripture, and awaken every morning during your journey toward healing and wholeness to recite these words: *"This is the day the Lord has made; let us rejoice and be glad in it"* (Psalm 118:24 HCSB). Remember, you awoke this morning, when a whole lot of people didn't.

Chapter 4

It's Gonna Take a While to Heal

Do not be anxious about anything, but in everything by prayer and supplication with thanksgiving let your requests be made known to God. (Philippians 4:6 ESV)

The sooner you accept the reality that it takes a long time to heal from severe trauma to your body, mind, or spirit, the better you will recover mentally and emotionally while navigating the arduous road you will travel toward healing and wholeness.

I told myself, "Self, it's going to take a while." However, I was not prepared for what this really meant. One month after surgery, I was having night sweats and painful spasms in my intestines and stomach. I was deprived of sleep. Food made me nauseated and put pressure on my infant stomach. It wasn't until this moment that I truly realized that it really was going to take a while before my body returned to health and wholeness.

My family and friends would say to me, "Rest and take it easy." Right! Telling a highly motivated, Type A person to take it easy is like telling the ocean to "keep from rushing to the shore. It's just impossible." Cue Perry Como singing, "It's Impossible." Nope! Can't take it easy. I was born in motion, and an object in motion remains in motion (See Newton's laws of motion). Of course, what one of Newton's laws states is "every object persists in its state of rest or uniform motion in a straight line unless it is compelled to change that state by forces impressed on it." Oops, those words "forces impressed on it" tend to compel change.

I learned an important thing about the human body. God built this mechanism into your brain that will tell your body, "I will slow you down, if you don't pay attention to me and take care of yourself!" This is exactly what happened to me. During my convalescence, I began to experience fatigue, even while sitting at my computer trying to do work. As a result, I was compelled to slow down and rest. I sat down on the sofa one afternoon, after feeling fatigued while concentrating on my work. I literally fell over asleep, and woke up an hour later.

Take care of yourself, physically and emotionally. It takes a lot of energy to overcome physical or emotional pain due to trauma of any kind. It is draining and can have a very strong emotional impact on you.

During your healing, you are vulnerable. Try not to put yourself in situations that make you more susceptible to stress, which can drive you into a downward emotional spiral. Entertaining negative thinking or unnecessarily putting yourself in stressful situations will deplete your energy, which could very likely cause you to descend into the doldrums of depression and inhibit healing.

Do not allow negative thoughts to take root in your mind. Don't create negative stories in your mind regarding your condition and the terrible things that *could* happen but have not happened. Negative thoughts create a drama in your daydreaming with a cast of characters that perform a tragic theatrical play on the stage of your mind. Negative thoughts will cause you to spiral downward: "I'm sick, my dog died, the cat ate my gold fish," and so on.

If your thinking is starting to remind you of lyrics to a sad country song, then it is time for you to write some new positive lyrics, unless you think you are writing the next greatest country hit—not!

I know Mark Wright, a songwriter and country music producer in Nashville. He wrote the song, "She Got the Car. I Got the Shaft!" Okay, granted, you may feel like you were run over by a Mack truck and you have the shaft embedded in your psyche to prove it, but in the midst of your circumstances, express gratitude to God that, indeed, you woke up this morning, when a whole lot of people didn't. Thank God you are alive and breathing His breath of life.

Scripture admonishes and encourages us not to be anxious about anything, *"but in everything by prayer and supplication with thanksgiving let your requests be made known to God"* (Philippians 4:6 ESV). You might say, "I've been there and done that." Well, do it again! This time pray with *thanksgiving* in you heart, like you truly mean it.

Surround yourself with positive influences and positive people. Change the channel on the TV set if the station you are watching is a constant grind of negative news or, even worse, features a program or talk-show host that stirs your anger. Listen to music to sooth and comfort you (and I'm not talking about the blues). Pray. Read your Bible. Pray some more. Read a book. Whatever positive influences help you heal, think about these positive things.

Under normal circumstances, it is difficult to ingest and digest a steady diet of negative influences without creating some degree of nausea in your spirit. When you are ill or recovering from a traumatic experience of any kind, your emotions are exposed like raw nerve endings. You will need your energy for healing and spiritual strength. So, don't let negative influences drain you of the precious energy you will need to restore your health.

When you are feeling anxious and downtrodden or are struggling to keep your equilibrium to make it through the day, take your requests to God, so you may feel His presence.

You may not recognize God's presence at this moment during a struggle in your life. Ask God to help you realize His presence. Once you do, it will begin to calm your emotions, and you will experience peace that only God can give.

After Paul exhorted the Philippians to seek God through prayer with a spirit of thanksgiving, he gave them homework to do to help guard their hearts and minds:

Finally, brothers, whatever is true, whatever is honorable, whatever is just, whatever is pure, whatever is lovely, whatever is commendable, if there is any excellence, if there is anything worthy of praise, think about these things. (Philippians 4:8-9 ESV)

Once you have taken your concerns to God in prayer, don't go back to focus on thoughts that will drag you down. Do what Paul instructed the Philippians to do: Chart a course of positive thinking.

Meditation

Make a list of positive things for contemplation to help direct your thoughts in an upward, rather than downward, direction. The apostle Paul has already started the list. Now, write on a piece of paper the things in your life that are honorable, just, pure, lovely commendable, excellent, worthy of praise (continue the list), and "think about these things." Then, the next time the cast of negative characters step out onto the stage of your mind and begin to recite the tragic drama of hopelessness or doom and gloom in your life, pull out the list you have made of the things that point you in the direction of hope, healing, and wholeness, and recite these things out loud while looking at yourself in a mirror.

It's Gonna Take a While to Heal

After you have made your list of "positive things," read the following lyrics Julie Andrews sang in the great classic film, *The Sound of Music*. You may even find yourself singing the words as you read the lyrics:

"My Favorite Things"
Lyrics: Rodgers and Hammerstein
(*From The Sound of Music*)

*Raindrops on roses and whiskers on kittens,
bright copper kettles and warm woolen mittens,
brown paper packages tied up with strings,
these are a few of my favorite things.*

Cream colored ponies and crisp apple strudels, door bells and sleigh bells and schnitzel with noodles, wild geese that fly with the moon on their wings, these are a few of my favorite things.

Girls in white dresses with blue satin sashes, snowflakes that stay on my nose and eyelashes, silver white winters that melt into springs, these are a few of my favorite things.

When the dog bites, when the bee stings, when I'm feeling sad,

Journey to Healing & Cherry Popsicles Too

*I simply remember my favorite things,
and then I don't feel so bad.*

"My Favorite Things" Copyright © 1959 by Richard Rodgers and Oscar Hammerstein II. Copyright Renewed WILLIAMSON MUSIC, an Imagem Company, owner of publication and allied rights throughout the World. International Copyright Secured.
All Rights Reserved Used by Permission.

What are your favorite things? Think about these things, as you visualize good health and wholeness for yourself, physically, emotionally, and spiritually.

Parenthetically, doctors tell us that meditation with visualization of tranquil places or tranquil thoughts not only helps calm our spirits and relieve our stress, but these moments of meditation and positive visualizations also help reduce the intensity of pain.

Visualize a beach, or a walk in a park down a path engulfed with a canopy of tall trees, or a green field in early spring with snow capped mountains in the distance—whatever place or happy circumstance works for you. Close your eyes. Allow your breathing to deepen and rest in the moment, as you visualize a place of serenity with a prayer of thanksgiving in your heart.

Chapter 5

Gratitude

For I know the plans I have for you, declares the Lord, plans for welfare and not for evil, to give you a future and a hope. (Jeremiah 29:11 ESV)

Nike made popular the slogan: "Just do it." So, let's get it in gear and do it. Here we go.

I'm not suggesting you put on your Nike running shoes and run a marathon or lift a thousand pounds at the gym, especially if you are recovering from surgery or some major illness. What I am suggesting is that if you do not begin every day with gratitude and thanksgiving in your heart, then like an athlete in training, strap on the power of positive thinking and lace it up with the power of prayer, then you *will* experience gratitude and thanksgiving in your heart. "Just do it."

Even if you don't feel like it, just do it. Even if it feels hypocritical to you, because frankly you don't feel well, still, just do it.

God has declared for you and me that His plans for us are "not for evil," but, rather, for our "welfare" to give us "a future and a hope." My heart overflows with joyful thanksgiving, because Jesus paid the price for my sins. He hung on a cross and died for you and me and then rose victorious over sin, death, and the grave to assure our eternal future. The future and hope God "declares" for us are not temporal; they are eternal through Jesus Christ, our Savior and Lord, by the power of His resurrection.

You may struggle with finding your prayer of thanksgiving. How about quoting a favorite Bible verse? Use your favorite scripture(s), a hymn, or a spiritual poem as a prayer of thanksgiving to guide you into a state of contemplative gratitude. If you don't have *something* that focuses your attention on gratitude and thanksgiving to God, no matter your circumstances, then read Jeremiah 29:11. This should do it. So, just do it.

Gratitude to God for This Precious Gift of Life Is the Pathway Toward Healing and Wholeness.

Once I finally returned home from the hospital, it was a challenge to tolerate food. I still had an eighteen-inch bypass tube implanted into my stomach, which dangled from beneath my loosely fitting T-shirt. The lack of strength to bathe exhausted me. My stomach and intestines certainly did not play well together, as they were in their infancy of regenerating any semblance of bowel and intestinal normalcy. I recall awakening many mornings after alternating between pain and light sleep during extremely restless nights. Sometimes the nights were so painful I had to wipe away the tears, as I lay in bed with groans and moans that only God could understand. I recall my body shaking and shallow breathing and panting induced by pain, but the temptation to focus only on my pain was lessened when I prayed a prayer of gratitude, even through tears.

You can dwell on your circumstances when you feel down, and if you are not careful, your less than pleasant circumstances can lead you down a spiraling path away from healing and deeper into depression. Yes, it is normal to feel down when you are sick, or downtrodden due to some form of trauma in your life, but gratitude will lead you back to rejuvenated life.

Gratitude Is a Key to Healing. Follow Its Path.

Thank you, God, that Your presence is with me in every breath I take and that You are healing my spirit, even though my body is hurting.

Meditation 1

Acknowledge God's presence through the trembling in your soul, your anxiety, and even in the shallowness of your breath. Consciously slow your shallow breathing with deep and elongated breaths as you inhale. Slowly exhale as you offer thanks to God for each breath of life you take. Do this meditative exercise for five minutes every day. Then, count your blessings. Name them one by one.

"Count Your Blessings"
Words: Johnson Oatman, Jr., 1897

When upon life's billows you are tempest tossed,
When you are discouraged, thinking all is lost,
Count your many blessings name them one by one,

Gratitude

And it will surprise you what the Lord hath done.

Are you ever burdened with a load of care?
Does the cross seem heavy you are called to bear?
Count your many blessings, ev'ry doubt will fly,
And you will be singing as the days go by.

So, amid the conflict, whether great or small,
Do not be discouraged, God is over all;
Count your many blessings, angels will attend,
Help and comfort give you to your journey's end.

Count your blessings, name them one by one:
Count your many blessings see what God hath done;
Count your blessings, name them one by one;
Count your many blessings see what God hath done.

Copyright: Public Domain
Hymns For His Praise: Number 2 Revised, 1906

Meditation 2

"Sit" with the following thought for a moment:
I am convinced that a grateful heart is God's
healing balm during the journey of my
recovery toward
healing and wholeness.

Write the above statement on a piece of paper or a sticky note, and place it where you will see it in your home or in a prominent place at work to encourage you throughout the day. Post it on the mirror in your bathroom, or attach it with a magnet to the front of your refrigerator. Just do it.

Know that you are enveloped by the loving presence of God's grace! Give thanks!

Chapter 6

Thanksgiving Day

Enter His gates with thanksgiving and His courts with praise. Give thanks to Him and praise His name. (Psalm 100:4 HCSB)

Today is Thanksgiving! Usually when I awaken on Thanksgiving Day, the anticipation of the Macy's Thanksgiving Day Parade streams into my consciousness. I can hardly wait for the parade to begin! I turn on my large-screen TV and jack up the volume on my surround-sound system. I love to hear the Christmas music as the marching high school bands play with much pride and gusto at center stage directly in front of the Macy's department store marquis, which is all decked out for Christmas. The floats, balloons, dancers,

Journey to Healing & Cherry Popsicles Too

Broadway and pop singers, the cheers and delight of a joyful crowd, and, of course, the grand arrival of good old St. Nick exude, jump, pop, swing, and teem with life.

What a thrilling way to kick off the holiday season! What a thrilling way to begin the day—everyday—with thanksgiving!

On this Thanksgiving Day, I awoke with great joy and gratitude as I breathed my first conscious breath: "I am alive!" I prayed a prayer of gratitude, as words began to enter my awaking consciousness. It was a simple prayer: "Thank you, God, for this precious gift of life." Immediately, a song of praise followed my simple prayer of gratitude: *"This is the day the Lord has made; let us rejoice and be glad in it"* (Psalm 118:24 HCSB).

On this most glorious of mornings in my awakened state, I thought to myself, "Six weeks ago I returned home from the hospital, feeble and frail. Yet, I awoke this morning with the realization that every day I live, breathe, and heal is a day of thanksgiving.

Help me, O God, to live this day with *thanks living*.

When we breathe those very first breaths of life at the dawning of each day, we experience the greatest gift of all, the gift of life, as God breathes into us His sustaining breath of life. We are reborn with our waking to experience a new day of life as a living soul. Each and every breath we take comes from the most holy and sacred place of God's being. We must never take this precious gift for granted, as every moment of our existence is a God-breathed miracle of grace.

My spirit wells up within me as I offer a sustained breath of gratitude to God for this miracle of life He has given me this day, this present moment of awareness and life.

I am alive in the wellness and wholeness of God's presence. He continues to heal my brokenness, as I journey toward physical, emotional, and spiritual healing and wholeness. My spirit lifts heavenward. I am undaunted by my physical circumstances, as my heart overflows with joyful thanksgiving.

It is God who woke me on this day of thanksgiving. It is God who is healing me physically and, more important, spiritually. It is God who has made a way for my healing from the sickness of sin to an eternal life of wholeness through the blood of the Lamb, His Son, Jesus Christ. I live and breathe in this moment with the assurance that regardless of my circumstances, it is well with my soul. God literally holds me in the palm of

His hand and in the presence of His eternal love and grace.

Thank You, Jesus! Thank You, Jesus! Thank You, my Lord and Savior!

His healing presence is with you too!

Yes, I will enjoy the fanfare of the Macy's Thanksgiving Day Parade today. This, too, is life to me; but the parade of Thanksgiving in my heart on this day of Thanksgiving pauses at the center stage of God's throne, as I kneel before His presence with gratitude for this precious gift of life. This is my greatest joy!

My body is healing, because a cheering crowd of spectators surrounds me—a throng of spiritual witnesses and prayer warriors. They continue to offer prayers to God for my healing. It is this bond that binds us together in the oneness of Christ, as we are enveloped and wrapped in the loving arms of God's mercy and grace.

I live! I breathe! My soul is well and rejoices! Today, and every day we live is a day of Thanksgiving. Let us rejoice and be glad in it!

Meditation

"It Is Well with My Soul"
Horatio G. Spafford, 1873

Thanksgiving Day

When peace, like a river, attendeth my way,
When sorrows like seas billows roll;
Whatever my lot, Thou hast taught me to say,
It is well, it is well with my soul.

Tho' Satan should buffet, tho' trials should come,
Let this blest assurance control,
That Christ has regarded my helpless estate,
And hath shed His own blood for my soul.

My sin – O, the bliss of this glorious tho't:
My sin not in part, but the whole,
Is nailed to the cross and I bear it no more,
Praise the Lord, praise the Lord, O my soul!

And, Lord, haste the day when the faith shall be sight,
The clouds be rolled back as a scroll,
The trump shall resound and the Lord shall descend,
Even so, it is well with my soul.

Copyright: Public Domain
Faith Publishing House, *Echoes from Heaven*, 1976

Take a slow, deep breath. Feel your lungs expand with renewed life. As you exhale, offer a prayer of thanksgiving to God: "Thank you, God, for breathing into me Your breath of life."

Repeat this exercise for as long as you feel the need to do so. Keep in mind that gratitude is a healing balm during the process of your recovery. It will humbly usher you to the throne of God's loving grace.

Chapter 7
Running a Marathon

But they that wait upon the Lord shall renew their strength; they shall mount up with wings as eagles; they shall run and not be weary; and they shall walk, and not faint. (Isaiah 40:31 KJV)

It was several months before Dr. Yachimski, a digestive disease physician at Vanderbilt University Medical Center in Nashville allowed me to go back to the gym to work out. I was chomping at the bit to return to the gym to help regain my strength and stamina. Finally, Dr. Yachimski gave me the go-ahead to do cardiovascular training in "moderation." I knew the definition of the word, but I would more fully discover its pragmatic meaning once I began my new workout regimen.

I could hardly wait to step onto the elliptical machine in the gym. However, it didn't take long to realize that while the first day back in the gym was a significant milestone in my quest to return to improved health and wholeness, it certainly was not a record-setting day in terms of preparing to break the world record in the marathon. Nevertheless, I mounted the elliptical to slowly begin my cardiovascular workout. I did it—very slowly—and I survived the day.

After about a month of a disciplined cardiovascular workout, I began to feel more confident that the crest of the hill I was climbing toward recovery was obtainable. Dr. Yachimski still did not want me to do any weight lifting, which was just fine with me, because I certainly didn't want to tear something apart inside my body. Simply pushing the treads up and down on that wonderful elliptical machine, as the wheel spun round and round, was one of those nuggets of healing that before my surgery I had taken for granted.

One day while I was slowly and methodically working the treads on the elliptical machine, two women decided to work out beside me—or I should say, mostly talk, while slowly making the wheel of the elliptical spin.

I was huffing and puffing and lost my focus when the topic of the women changed from the latest hairstyles to the upcoming Nashville Marathon, less than a month away. One of the women said to her workout partner that she had suffered an injury but felt well enough to train for the marathon. The other woman next to me had a cast on her left foot, which extended up her leg and stopped just below her knee. Not to be outdone, she said to her workout friend, "I think I will run in the Nashville Marathon too."

My brain screamed with laughter in response, "Yeah! Right!" Fortunately, my mouth didn't articulate the words or laughter in my brain. However, I couldn't keep from staring at the woman in the leg cast, thinking, "Are you kidding me? Really? The Nashville Marathon is less than a month away, you're in a cast, and you think somehow you're going to begin training today and run a 26.2-mile marathon next month? I don't think so."

Admittedly, my athletic days of many years past were reminding me of the discipline and focused training it took for me to remain competitive. I was on the cross-country team in high school in addition to playing basketball as one of the starting five; and I played other sports. Also, I conditioned myself in college and graduate school to run long distances.

While I know there are some wonderful stories about people overcoming incredible physical limitations to perform great feats of athleticism, it takes discipline, patience, time, and focused rehabilitation for most of us who have suffered injury or a severe illness to heal. It often takes much time and effort simply to get back to a state of physical (and emotional) normalcy.

After all, I overcame great odds to live after suffering a major blockage in my intestines that caused "stomach death," but running a marathon with only one month of training was absolutely ridiculous to consider except in my dreams, and I had doubts about that.

Sometimes, we need to have an attitude adjustment to express gratitude for our progressive recovery, even if we will not conceivably have the capability to run a metaphorical marathon in the near future.

Nevertheless, as someone who trained athletically for competitive sports, I know the importance of allowing *time* for bones and muscles to heal following an injury, prior to "running a marathon," so as not to risk greater injury.

Sure, I could have defied the doctor's instructions not to lift weights, simply to prove him wrong when he said, "Only do cardiovascular exercising in moderation." However, tearing apart my organs that were recently stitched back together was something I did not want to experience. Needlessly exposing myself to potential injury would have led to more serious long-term consequences and healing problems, had I given into my ego rather than listened to common sense.

Additionally, building physical strength, stamina, and endurance takes discipline and focused training for many months to achieve the physical condition required to run a few miles, let alone, a 26.2-mile marathon. Serious marathon athletes train for years. There was no way I could see how the woman working out next to me *with a cast on her foot* could properly train to run a 26.2-mile race in less than one month.

Hopefully, you realize by now that I had come face to face with my own lack of ability to run even a mile, as a result of "eavesdropping" on a conversation between two women who were planning to train and run in a marathon in less than a month.

Okay, this encounter was not about these women training for a marathon. It was, plain and simple, about my own impatience in wanting to be physically where I was not and could not be at this moment in time.

Oh, how I wish I could have fast-forwarded one year into the future, but I was stuck in the present moment, where I should have been dwelling in the first place with gratitude in my heart for the progress of my own recovery, rather than wishing for something at this moment that was not possible. These ladies provided me with a dose of reality I had to swallow, while listening to them entertain me as they worked out beside me in the gym. Mercifully, a comforting scripture came to mind:

But they that wait upon the Lord shall renew their strength; they shall mount up with wings as eagles; they shall run and not be weary; and they shall walk, and not faint. (Isaiah 40:31 KJV)

I privately said a prayer to myself in that very moment: "Thank you, God, that I am on the road to recovery, and my body is healing! Help me to wait upon you, as you are renewing my strength and making me whole. I am confident I will once again mount up with wings as eagles, run and not be weary, and walk without fainting. I'm getting there, day by day, one step and one Blue Bell Cherry Popsicle at a time. But, I ain't runnin' no marathon today!"

Stop reading for a moment, and offer God a prayer of gratitude for His presence with you during the process of your healing, whether physically, emotionally, or spiritually. Then, after a few moments of silence, continue reading.

As I continued to exercise, I decided to put my workout on autopilot and listen to the women beside me, as they continued to provide me with entertainment.

Don't get me wrong. I'm all for confidence in setting goals, but I thought to myself, I couldn't imagine running a marathon, or even a half marathon, in six months or even a year after what I had been through. Yes, I know this was my baggage, but understand that I was in top shape before surgery and had conditioned myself for many years.

A third woman showed up, an obvious friend of the two marathon-bound women training beside me on elliptical machines. As the two ladies greeted her, the conversation turned into a three-way social gathering for the trio.

By now my speed on the elliptical had surpassed the marathon-bound women-in-training, even though my mother could have beaten me on this day, and she was in her eighties at the time.

The woman in the cast blurted out, "Pat, I am so glad you are here. I just have to tell you that the Snickers Cake you gave me was so delicious. I must get the recipe from you."

So, let me get this straight. The woman in the cast was going to train and run in a marathon that was less than a month away, while enjoying her "Snickers Cake" during her training for the big event. I literally burst into laughter.

I don't know the end to this story, but it caused me to think, "How realistic am I about my progress?" I had already come to grips with the fact that it was going to take a while for my body and spirit to become whole again. Nevertheless, I reminded myself to exercise patience, as I exercised my body, and not become frustrated because I was not healing as fast as I had hoped. Yet, the doctors were telling me I was ahead of schedule in terms of healing and that I was doing remarkably well. Still, I needed to *"wait upon the Lord."*

I am a competitive person, but had I unrealistically tried to push beyond my limitations (which could have physically harmed me), then discouragement easily could have overtaken me. I'm all for pushing the envelope (this can also be a problem for me with some negative consequences), but during the process of healing, unrealistic fantasies and grandiose expectations are *not* helpful! They can discourage us.

Your body will heal in its own time. Listen to your doctors! Listen to your body! Stop listening to someone who does not walk in your shoes during your journey toward healing and wholeness!

Put off thinking about running that marathon for another day, when it is more realistic to consider. Keep in mind that you are already engaged in a marathon, a marathon toward healing and wholeness. Even if you never run that marathon race due to your lack of physical capabilities, simply *live* in gratitude and offer gratitude to God for the progress of your healing and the health you have this day that allows you to live and breathe God's wondrous breath of life.

Even though you may struggle through pain and feel faint, wait on the Lord. Be patient. He will renew your strength. You are making progress toward healing and wholeness. Live into your life just as it is, and experience it one step, one day, and one Blue Bell Cherry Popsicle at a time.

Meditation 1

Claim this scripture for your life:
Hast thou not known? Hast thou not heard, that the everlasting God, the Lord, the Creator of the ends of the earth, fainteth not, neither is weary?

There is no searching of His understanding. He giveth power to the faint; and to them that have no might he increaseth strength. Even the youths shall faint and be weary, and the young men shall utterly fall: **but they that wait upon the Lord shall renew their strength; they shall mount up with wings as eagles; they shall run and not be weary; and they shall walk; and not faint.** (Isaiah 40:28-31 KJV)

Meditation 2

Remember the three steps to guide us as we walk together toward healing and wholeness discussed in the introduction of this book? Read them again and contemplate them before you continue reading:

Step One: **Have a positive attitude focused on directness of purpose and a resolve rooted in gratitude for life**. Resist the temptation to give in to the distraction of your pain, which you know is there, and perhaps is constant during your recovery.

Step Two: **Recognize the little things in your life that encourage hope during the process of your healing and recovery**—like a Blue Bell Cherry Popsicle. Try to recognize even the smallest kernel of hope in the midst of your pain. What is YOUR symbolic Blue Bell Cherry Popsicle that encourages hope?

Step Three: **Offer a prayer of gratitude and thanksgiving for the rays of hope you discover along the path of your healing during the journey.** Have an *attitude of gratitude.*

Chapter 8

Limited LifeTIME Warranty—Uncertainty and Blessings

Father, if you are willing, take this cup away from me—nevertheless, not my will but yours, be done. (Luke 22:42 HCSB)

Even when you do not realize it, you are blessed. You may not *feel* blessed at this moment, given your circumstances. Perhaps you don't feel your process of healing has begun or your convalescence is not going well. Nevertheless, you are blessed.

I realize that life on earth has a limited lifeTIME warranty that comes with exclusions that are unique to every individual, given our circumstances; but in the loving arms of God through Jesus Christ, you have an eternal life warranty. Notice the word *time* does not appear in "eternal life."

Unlike a limited lifeTIME warranty, which expires at death, an eternal life warranty recorded in the Book of Life through the saving grace of Jesus Christ does not expire—time does not exist in eternity. There is no need for a limited lifeTIME warranty, because through Jesus Christ we live and have life in the eternal presence of God through His grace. We are blessed. You are blessed.

No, I do not presume to know your circumstances. You could say right about now that you are miserable, hurting, depressed, and forsaken and that I have no idea what you are going through. You are right. I don't know your circumstances, and while I cannot walk in your shoes, I too have felt forsaken, alone, and depressed and have hurt in numerous ways, but I am blessed.

Connect with me for a moment as I share with you one of the more painful moments in my life that even supersedes my own near-death experience and difficult recovery.

My joy and peace of mind were assaulted by a traumatic illness that threatened my son's life.

Limited LifeTIME Warranty—Uncertainty and Blessings

The long and arduous journey required for his survival made it extremely difficult to see God's blessings in my life, as I struggled to help my son survive what perhaps is a parent's worst nightmare. "Your son has cancer. There is no cure. We will do all we can."

Ten days before our son's fourteenth birthday, Emily and I received devastating news from an orthopedic oncologist that Kyle Jr. had osteosarcoma, which is a rare and incurable form of bone cancer that primarily invades and devastates the lives of teens while ravaging the body.

The next year of our lives was one of the worst and most difficult experiences our family has endured. Kyle Jr. was administered highly toxic doses of chemotherapy with side effects that jeopardized his life even further. It was incredible the number of side effects patients experience from the type of chemotherapy Kyle Jr. had to endure.

As a result of the chemotherapy administered to him, Kyle Jr. suffered kidney damage and a partial loss of hearing. Neutropenia severely weakened his immune system during his chemotherapy treatments. His body constantly experienced bacterial attacks, causing infections. Without megadoses of antibiotics administered intravenously to him in the hospital and at home, Kyle Jr. would have died, due to a suppressed immune system.

Between the chemotherapy treatments, emergency admissions to the hospital, and several surgeries, we spent an entire year living mostly at the hospital with our son at Georgetown University Medical Center in Washington, D.C.

During that year, after several months of induction chemotherapy, Kyle Jr. had to undergo surgery to remove his cancerous right hip and upper femur. It was a very serious surgery that took eight hours to complete in addition to several hours in recovery for stabilization.

The surgeon, who was an orthopedic oncologist, designed and implanted a titanium prosthetic hip and upper femur in Kyle Jr.'s body. The modular-designed hip and limb were uniquely designed prosthetics. The process of implantation was what the surgeon called "limb-sparing surgery." After surgery, our son looked like the Bionic Kid on X-ray film with a titanium hip and femur that were fused with the remaining bones in his right leg.

The pain of healing from the orthopedic surgery was unmerciful. I stayed in the intensive care unit by Kyle Jr.'s bedside and did not sleep for three days. Emily and I took shifts attending the needs of our son. I recall never leaving the hospital

Limited LifeTIME Warranty—Uncertainty and Blessings

during the most crucial and critical time after Kyle Jr.'s surgery, as his health worsened and his body weakened.

As the days turned into months, I began to learn the names of the children in the pediatric oncology ward. I recall on one occasion looking around the ward and noticing that all the children were beginning to look alike to me. They all had baldheads, no eyebrows, no hair on their entire body; and the children looked anorexic, due to their chemotherapy treatments. Some of the children had open sores. Other children vomited uncontrollably. Some of them died during that year, which broke my heart.

Something happened to me during those months of encounters with extremely ill children. I still recall their angelic faces after more than two decades. The thought of gravely ill children continues to stir my emotions to this day.

I watched adult visitors to the pediatric oncology ward recoil with fear upon seeing the sores and baldheads of these sick children, as if they were shielding and embracing themselves with folded arms in disbelief that these little ones could suffer so much.

I came face to face with my own mortality through the fragility of life my son and these children with cancer were experiencing.

Yet, at that very moment, even at the darkest hour, I realized what a blessing life is. I was blessed with life, my life, as well as the presence of my wife and two beautiful children. The pain I felt for our son, who was struggling to survive at that moment, reminded me how precious life is! I was very much aware that God had granted Emily and me His grace gifts of our son and daughter. I was also aware that those moments were filled with uncertainty and the horrifying thought that I might outlive our son, a dastardly thought that I was forced to consider. I so desperately wanted healing and wholeness for Kyle Jr.

The paradox was experiencing gratitude for life during the death threat of cancer, while watching my son and other sick children suffer.

Nevertheless, I began to thank God, through tears of grief, for this great gift of life He granted me with every breath I breathed; and for whatever time our son had left, I thanked God for His goodness in granting Emily and me the precious gift of Kyle Jr.'s life.

Compassion began to replace my fears, and instead of recoiling and disengaging from the sickness that surrounded me, I began to interact more with the children in the pediatric oncology ward at Georgetown University Medical Center. On one occasion, I knelt beside a young girl in a wheelchair who had many sores all over her body. Crusts had formed on her skin as a result of her open and oozing sores that had tattooed both of her arms. I recall talking to her, rather than ignoring her or acting like she wasn't there. My focus became a compassionate gaze rather than a coy stare. I looked at her and saw her for who she was, a little girl who was afraid, even as I embraced my own fears. I no longer saw the sores, or the wheelchair, or her baldhead. Rather, I saw and touched a little girl who simply needed someone around her not to fear her because she was sick.

So we talked. I talked to her about her cancer. After all, it was the "big elephant in the room." I asked her how she felt. She took the opportunity to tell me how she felt and what she thought about her cancer without the projection of my fears erupting from facing my own mortality through my son's illness.

The next several years were difficult for Kyle Jr. as they were filled with rehabilitation and cancer treatment protocols with constant tests and follow-up visits to oncologists. He had to learn how to walk all over again, which required much physical therapy to ascertain that he was strong enough to walk steadily with his implanted limb-sparring prosthesis.

After a period of nine years in remission, Kyle Jr. relapsed the summer after graduating from Belmont University in Nashville. His osteosarcoma had returned, not to the primary site in his right leg and hip, but to his right lung. He was given a 5 percent chance of recovery from the metastasized cancer, which required additional surgery to remove one-third of his right lung. No additional chemotherapy was administered, as it was deemed ineffective at that time. At this point, Kyle Jr. had outlived all the other children diagnosed with osteosarcoma at the same time he was treated at Georgetown University Medical Center in Washington, D.C.

I was devastated! However, my life had changed over the years. Yes, I told God in no uncertain terms that I didn't want to outlive my son! And as I broke, instead of bitterness, my heart returned to gratitude, even during my saddest laments.

I was at an odd place of awareness, experiencing great grief and trauma, while having a profound sense of gratitude for life, as it was unfolding during those moments of great despair. Once again, I thanked God for the blessings He gave me and my family in granting Emily and me our two most precious gifts, our son and daughter.

That little girl in the wheelchair, Jason who died, and the other children I knew by name who did not survive, children whose precious presence are still with me today—I thanked God for those precious lives. I came to realize that while those beautiful children had a limited lifeTIME warranty (and their lives were far too short for my human understanding), they no longer suffered and now abide in the eternal arms and loving presence of God.

I did not want our son to suffer. Yet I needed to express to God my truest feelings, which I did with great emotion. Then I prayed like Christ prayed as He faced the prospect of His death hanging in loneliness on a cross: *"Father, if you are willing, take this cup away from me—nevertheless, not My will, but Yours, be done"* (Luke 22:42 HCSB).

The paradox is that I had not given up on my son. What I did was surrender his eternal well-being to God's grace. Then, Emily and I resolved to do everything humanly possible to support our son, come hell or high water!

Surrendering to God's ultimate will does not mean we are to give up. Surrender simply means that when we've done everything humanly possible to support life, there will come a time for all of us, young and old alike, when we will face death as our limited lifeTIME warranty expires. We will cross over the threshold of death into the eternal loving presence of God, who suspends time and welcomes us into the presence of His eternal love and grace.

Kyle Jr., has had the blessing of two decades of life beyond his initial diagnosis of incurable cancer. I often reflect on the children, who, unlike my son, have long since passed away. I don't have the answer to the number of years God grants us life on this earth. We all know that some people are given many more years of life than others.

Sickness and tragedies claim the lives of loved ones, and it is all far beyond what we can understand with our limited human capacities; but God heals all of us, sometimes in this present life for a short while. As for the little ones I knew who suffered from cancer so many years ago in that pediatric oncology ward at Georgetown University Medical Center, God chose to heal those precious children in heaven, as He will do one day for you and me when time is no more.

Meditation

Even at death's door, the gateway to eternity, you are blessed. Reflect on the blessings in your life, while embracing your own mortality. Give thanks to God that in Jesus Christ, God will meet you at eternity's door when your physical life on earth ceases to exist.

CHAPTER 9

FLASHBACK

Even when I go through the darkest valley, I fear no danger, for You are with me. (Psalm 23:4 HCSB)

It was January 2012, approximately nine months before I became deathly ill. My cell phone rang. It was Kyle Jr. There was great trouble in his voice. He said, "Dad, I have some really bad news. My cancer has returned. It's in my bladder."

My heart sank! My brain went into automatic rewind mode as it flashed back to that dreadful day in 1993 when the orthopedic oncologist first broke the news to Emily and me that our son had osteosarcoma. There is no cure for this ravaging disease. Longevity after diagnosis is only five years, and Kyle Jr. had far outlived the national and international statistics on longevity.

Here we were again, battling the curse of our son's dreadful disease, nineteen years after he was first diagnosed with bone cancer and just five months before his triplet babies were born. It appeared that Kyle Jr.'s cancer had returned with a vengeance, as a tumor occupied his bladder.

Kyle Jr. left the urology oncologist's office with his mother. The cauliflower-shaped tumor was so invasive that it had punctured through the wall of his bladder and protruded out the bladder's exterior wall.

Kyle Jr. was visibly moved as he said to Emily, "I will never see my children grow up; and my wife will be left to raise our three children without me."

While Emily tried to comfort our son with her love and compassion, she was very direct, saying to him, "Kyle David, you've beaten cancer twice. You don't know how much time you have left. That's up to God."

This was not a time for superficial spiritualization or pontificating empty platitudes meant to anesthetize the reality of this desperate moment. It was a time for prayer and the presence of God through the brokenhearted love of a mother's embrace.

Flashback

Oh, how desperate we were for God's presence!

As I recalled that cold January day in 2012, I had few words of comfort for my son other than, "You are not alone. You are loved. We will pray."

My thoughts continued to bounce back and forth between May of 1993, when Kyle Jr. was first diagnosed with bone cancer, and January of 2012, that terrible day of contemplation that my son may never see his triplet babies grow up.

There was no joy in the days that followed the dreadful realization that Kyle Jr.'s cancer had metastasized to his bladder. This was the third time he would have to fight to survive this relentless disease.

Emily was contemplating taking family leave from Vanderbilt University Medical Center to take care of our son. Simultaneously, we were considering how to support Jenna, who must care for herself and her three unborn babies she was carrying in her womb in the midst of dealing with her husband's condition, which by all appearances was grave. All our family was totally devastated and absolutely exhausted by this trauma—physically, emotionally, and spiritually.

I recall walking into our son's home, soon after absorbing the shocking blow of his condition. I remember gazing at three empty baby cribs in the nursery that were colorfully decorated. A rocking chair was carefully placed in the corner of the room, and all the wonderful, delicate stuffed toys and baby things were awaiting the arrival of three beautiful bundles of joy—new life.

My heart broke, and I began to sob uncontrollably! Even as I share this story, my emotions are stirred. It was too much to bear, contemplating losing my son while longing to celebrate the joyful arrival of my three grandbabies!

How does one process these simultaneous thoughts of precious newborn life and of a disease that has ravaged my son's body for so many years?

The cognitive dissonance I experienced traumatized me. Trauma stacked on trauma had laid siege to my emotional, psychological, and spiritual well-being! There were no words! There were moans and groans in prayer! There was an unspeakable, desperate hope that God would somehow break through this harbinger of death! His merciful presence was needed to quell the all-consuming, paradoxical loneliness and despair and bring peace and comfort.

My mind swarmed with the cacophony of words the doctor shared with Kyle Jr. prior to his surgery: Only 30 percent of patients with bladder cancer of this advanced stage live three years. This

Flashback

is only after radical surgery that would require removing his bladder, prostate, and other surrounding organs. Major internal reconstruction of the urinary tract was required and most likely a colostomy with an external bag; and at the end of a very lengthy recovery from surgery *death*!

After Surgery

The surgeon cut out as much of the mass as possible from Kyle Jr.'s bladder. A biopsy was sent to the lab.

I was with Kyle Jr. in the recovery room when a nurse entered the room. He was awake and struggling after surgery. The nurse asked him if she could do anything for him. He responded by saying, "Yes, could you get me a new body?" Then, he said something I will never forget as long as I live. He immediately corrected himself, "No, I don't need a new body. I think my body has done a good job fighting this cancer."

It was at that moment in his hurting state, as he wondered whether or not he would live to see his triplet babies grow up, that Kyle Jr. displayed an incredible attitude of gratitude for his wonderful body.

He expressed gratitude in spite of the fact that he had suffered and nearly died from cancer nearly two decades earlier. He offered gratitude that his body helped him survive cancer, even nine years later, when his cancer spread to his right lung.

Indeed, Kyle Jr. was still alive and grateful that his body had found a way to sustain him throughout high school, college, marriage, and now that he was awaiting the birth of his triplet babies.

Things Are Not Always As They Appear!

Several days after Kyle Jr. left the hospital, he called me. There was joy in his voice. He said, "Dad, I just spoke with the surgeon. He said he can't explain what happened, and that he sees tumors like I have all the time. It looked like cancer, acted like cancer, and he thought my bone cancer or some other form of cancer had spread to my bladder; but, Dad, it's not cancer! The biopsy came back negative!"

What overcoming joy this news brought to my grieving heart!

Kyle Jr. continued to tell me the surgeon had called in several pathologists for a consultation. The physicians were so convinced this was an advanced stage of bladder cancer that the diagnosis was already entered into Kyle Jr.'s medical records. But, the biopsy showed that he did not have a cancerous tumor, and the pathologists were stunned!

The roller coaster of emotions at that moment caused my blood pressure to drop. I felt weak. The joy was overwhelming! Praise the Lord!

Kyle Jr. continued, "Dad, they don't know what to call it. I have to go back for another biopsy in six weeks. They want to make sure my cancer has not returned; but for now the surgeon is not going to touch any remaining parts of the tumor, because if they try to remove all of it, I would have a large hole in my bladder where the tumor has punctured through the wall of my bladder."

The second biopsy was even more promising. The tumor was shrinking. And then, just three days before the triplets were born, Kyle Jr. had one last checkup: There were no signs of the tumor. Kyle Jr.'s bladder had completely healed!

Fast-Forward

As the thoughts of my son's struggle with cancer invaded my consciousness during my own convalescence, I realized there was a reason I was experiencing this flashback. I was struggling with facing my own mortality. However, the painful difficulty in living day to day with my son's cancer for more than twenty years helped remind me that things are not always as they appear; and as my dear wife said to our son during one of his darkest moments, "You don't know how much time you have left. That's up to God." After all, while there is no cure for our son's cancer, and even though relapse has threatened his life, Kyle Jr. is still alive and is a very busy dad, I might add!

I too am alive at this very moment—breathing in God's breath of life—and so are you!

God is here for you and me during our struggles in the here and now. One day, He will come for us at the point of our need when it is time for us to meet Him at the door of eternity: *"Yea, though I walk through the valley of the shadow of death, I will fear no evil; for thou art with me"* (Psalm 23:4 KJV).

God's ultimate healing of our body, mind, and spirit is found in His eternal presence. Yet until we cross the threshold of this earthly life to eternal life, there is no doctor, no pastor, or anyone else who knows the date and time when God will escort us to our eternal home, where we will dwell in the presence of eternal love and grace forever! This is something I have learned during the past twenty plus years of gratitude for life during my son's illness and more especially now that I am on the road to healing and wholeness in my life.

God's eternal love and grace for me are ever present and unfolding as I awaken every morning to the newness of life. I remind myself of this during the days when life's circumstances cause me to struggle.

God's presence is with you too. Things are not always as they appear. Have faith that God's grace is unfolding in your life and that His loving presence is with you during your most desperate moments when you feel forsaken and alone.

Above all, live life with "thanks living"—living life with joyful gratitude, purpose, and meaning. Seek to make a positive difference in God's kingdom as you encounter family, friends, and strangers during your journey. Remember, you are living hope for someone in your concentric circles of influence.

The last chapter of your life is not written; and when that chapter begins, it is not the end, only the beginning of God's will for your life in eternity.

Meditation

Pause for a moment to thank God, once again, for His breath of life that sustains you, even through your pain and darkest moments. More important, thank God that when He meets you at the door of eternity, He will walk with you "through the valley of the shadow of death," into the glorious light of His loving presence for all eternity!

Chapter 10

Healing of the Soul

And God shall wipe away all tears from their eyes; and there shall be no more death, neither sorrow, nor crying, neither shall there be any more pain: For the former things are passed away. And he that sat upon the throne said, Behold, I make all things new. (Revelation 21:4-5 KJV)

One evening Emily said to me, "I'm reading a devotional book by a preacher whose name is Tony Campolo." I immediately respond by saying,

"I've met Tony Campolo. He spoke at Belmont University in Nashville a couple of years ago. I even got to eat lunch with him."

Emily continued, "Well he's written a devotional that you need to hear."

Before she continued with the story, Emily said to me, "When Kyle Jr. was first diagnosed with cancer, a lady asked me, 'What do you want us to pray for?'"

Emily recalled that she stood in front of the lady thinking for a minute, and then she responded, "Like anyone else who has a sick loved one, pray for healing; but if that's not in God's ultimate plan, then pray that Kyle Jr. will have such a dynamic experience with God that he will feel His presence as he walks through this experience."

Emily so desperately wanted healing for our son, but if God chose not to heal our son physically, she prayed for spiritual healing. She also prayed that our son would have the miraculous presence of God, so he would not feel alone.

It is against this backdrop and the realization that our physical lives will one day come to an end that Emily read to me the following devotional from Tony Campolo's book, *Stories that Feed Your Soul:*

Healing of the Soul

It was a dozen years ago that I was speaking at a Christian leaders' conference in South Africa.

The other speaker was a preacher named Randy Clark who undoubtedly had spiritual gifts that were truly amazing.

One morning when we were at breakfast, Randy asked me if I had a healing ministry. I responded by saying, "If you mean, do I pray for people when they are sick, the answer is yes, but to be perfectly honest, not much happens. But if you mean, do I conduct healing services like some of those televangelists do, the answer is no."

"Why not?" Randy asked. To this I responded, "Because, as I told you, nothing much happens when I pray for people to be healed."

With a smirk on his face, he said, "That hasn't kept you from preaching."

A couple of weeks later, I was in a Nazarene Church in Oregon. As I got up to speak, I noticed that there was a little bottle of olive oil on the ledge inside the pulpit. As soon as I saw it, I felt compelled to say to the congregation, "There is some oil here. If any of you would like to stay behind for a healing service, feel free to do so."

"But first, there are a couple of things I need to tell you. First, I can't be in a hurry. I will need to connect with each one of you, to talk with you and get a feel for what you are going through. That will probably mean taking at least a few minutes with each person who stays for healing. The second thing is that, to be honest, I am not a healer and I don't expect much to happen."

About thirty people came forward at the end of the service and sat in the first couple of pews, waiting for prayer. I prayed with each of them. To my surprise, most of them had nothing physically wrong w ith them. Depression was the major reason most of them came forward for prayer. Just a handful of them had serious physical ailments.

Two weeks later, I received a telephone call from a woman who told me that her husband had been one of those who came forward for prayer. She then went on to say that he had had cancer. When I heard the word "had" I was thrilled. "Had cancer?" I asked. "How is he now?"

"He died," was her response.

I didn't know what to say. I apologized. I said I was sorry. I stammered a bit.

Then she surprised me by saying, "I really called to thank you. Before that healing service, my husband was filled with anger against God and against everyone else. He was only 58 years old. He had hoped to see his grandchildren grow up. He would lie in bed and curse God. Nobody wanted to be around him, least of all me. But after you prayed, everything changed. The last two weeks we had together was the best time we ever had. We sang together and laughed together, and shared a time of incredible joy. If I had a choice between those last days and our last five years together, it would be no choice at all. Those last few days were so wonderful."

Then she said something profound, "He wasn't cured, but he was healed."

I thought about that for a long time. Any cure is only temporary. No matter what miracle takes place wherein God intercedes and cures someone of something that the doctors said was incurable, the reality is that eventually the person will die. Cures are only for a time, but the healing of the heart, the mind and the soul is forever. (*Stories That Feed Your Soul,* Regal, 146-147).

Tony Campolo. Stories That Feed Your Soul:
"Healing of the Soul."
Baker Books, a division of Baker Publishing Group.
Copyright © 2010. Used by permission.

Getting Beyond the Great Beyond

When you experience your own vulnerable mortality, it can shake you to the core of your being. At least this was the case for me. I have always experienced health, strength, and an abundance of energy and vitality for life. On one occasion while leading a choir and orchestra in rehearsal, the evening became later. I was jumping around and directing wildly. One of the men in the choir raised his hand.

"Yes, Louis. What is it?"

He responded, "If you could bag all that energy you have and sell it, you'd be the richest man on earth." Of course, the choir and orchestra hysterically laughed.

In retrospect, I now realize how all these years I have taken my "hyper energy," as my wife calls it, for granted.

Bumping up against my mortality is not new to me, as I have experienced it on several occasions during my son's struggle to survive cancer. However, knocking on death's door, experienced in my own destitute circumstances, scared me!

I reminded myself that had I died on that operating table in Foley, Alabama, God would have met me at the threshold of eternity with His loving arms opened wide. Nevertheless, while these thoughts offered me assurance and comfort, I had an adrenalin rush and a rejuvenated drive for wanting more than ever to live in the here and now in a way that I had never lived before. I could no longer take my health for granted. More important,

I could no longer take the blessing of this gift of life, or my dearest and most treasured loved ones, for granted.

I had come face to face with "the great beyond" and had to get beyond it to live my life to the fullest for the remaining days I have left on this earth.

I understand that one day physical healing and this temporal life will no longer sustain you or me, but as Tony Campolo reminds us, "Cures are only for a time, but the healing of the heart, the mind and the soul is forever."

Meditation

"No matter what miracle takes place wherein God intercedes and cures someone of something that the doctors said was incurable, the reality is that eventually the person will die" (Tony Campolo).

Pray for healing of your heart, mind, and soul. Pray that God will help you embrace your own mortality through the resurrected power of Jesus Christ. If you have not done so already, ask Jesus to transform your life as your Savior and Lord so that you may experience His love and grace for all of eternity. Amen.

During the two years I was convalescing and writing this book, several tragedies struck our family. First came the tragic death of my daughter-in-law's brother; then my mother died; and less than two months after my mother's death, my wife's sister died. Finally, as I finished the final pages of this book, death claimed the life of my sister-in-law's brother. The death of four family members, and especially my dear mother, once again brought me poignantly face to face with my own mortality.

Chapter 11

Tragedy

The Spirit helps us in our weakness. For we do not know what to pray for as we ought, but the Spirit himself intercedes for us with groanings too deep for words. (Romans 8:26 ESV)

Friday, December 7, 2012. Barrett's funeral is tomorrow. He was my daughter-in-law's brother. Barrett was only thirty-three years old. He died as a result of a tragic motorcycle accident last weekend.

On Monday (December 3, 2012), I stood beside Barrett's hospital bed in the trauma unit at Vanderbilt University Medical Center in Nashville. Barrett's parents, Robert and Leesa Wood; his brother, Beau; sister, Jenna; my son, Kyle Jr., and

I stood silently with great sadness and grief as we encircled Barrett's hospital bed and gazed at his broken body, which could no longer sustain life.

How difficult it was in those moments to acknowledge and accept the sad truth that Barrett's life on this earth had come to a shockingly unexpected and tragic end. There were no words as we stood at Barrett's desperate bedside, only silent groanings within our individual spirits.

My spirit cried out for our family and for myself, "*Kyrie Eleison! Christe Eleison! Kyrie Eleison (Lord, have mercy! Christ, have mercy! Lord, have mercy!)!*"

It is with great difficulty during earth-shattering, tumultuous moments, when death surprises life as unsuspecting prey, that we try to gather our senses, our thoughts, and any sense of understanding of such a tragic loss—a loved one ripped from our presence! In these moments, in the absence of words, only God can comfort our pain. "Lord, have mercy! Christ, have mercy! Lord, have mercy!"

As tears gave way to intermittent silence, the prelude to words began with an embrace, followed by more tears, and an irreverent silence; but it still was not time to speak.

Thoughts of life's fragility flooded my mind. In the death of Barrett, I experienced a renewed sense

Tragedy

of my own near-death experience just two months earlier. I grieved the loss of Barrett, while thanking God for the lives of all my extended family members, who breathe and live, as together we will walk through this "valley of the shadow of death."

We may, indeed, experience our own mortality and the fragility of life in our times of great need and in the passing of a loved one. Parents sometimes must bury their child. There was no sickness, but death came to Barrett in such a tragically unexpected way.

Random thoughts and numerous questions threatened to cloud my mind. There were no satisfying answers to "Why, Lord Jesus? Why?" There are always questions behind questions, and we must not get stuck or mired in a quagmire of obsession to understand what only God can answer in the fullness of time in His eternal, loving presence. There are no spiritual platitudes at this moment that can comfort—only God's presence.

Yet even in the midst of grief, hope emerged! Barrett knew the Lord while living on this earth. He now knows God's presence of eternal love and life unending that has no pain or suffering.

When I could finally speak through my tears, I hugged Barrett's father, Robert, and said (for my sake and his), "Nothing can separate us from the love of God." I continued with Scripture. It was the hope I needed to remind myself that all was not lost!

For I am persuaded, that neither death, nor life, nor angels, nor principalities, nor powers, nor things present, nor things to come, nor height, nor depth, nor any other creature, shall be able to separate us from the love of God, which is in Christ Jesus our Lord. (Romans 8:38-39 KJV)

Death does not hold the final answer to eternity. God holds eternity in the palm of His hand, and it is by His grace that we are saved through faith in Jesus Christ for all eternity (Ephesians 2:8).

I closed my eyes just for a moment to contemplate this magnificent thought. I breathed in a deep, cleansing breath of life, and exhaled a prayer of thanksgiving in my heart for the life of Robert Barrett Wood. Then I moved around the bedside to gently touch Barrett and to say a prayer over his fatal and mortal brokenness for which there was no cure in this present life.

As I looked up from the bedside, I caught the eyes of Jenna, my daughter-in-law. My mind raced back to when my daughter, Keli, and Jenna were children.

Keli and Jenna were best friends as children, long before my son ever took notice or interest in

Tragedy

stealing Keli's friend and companion away from her to make Jenna his wife. I hugged Jenna, recalling her playfulness with Keli when they were young children. I told Jenna that a few years before she knew Keli, I lost my Grandmother Duvall. Keli was very close to her great-grandmother. She saw her daily and enjoyed many chats while eating snacks with her. I shared with Jenna the story of how Keli responded when I broke the news to her that Grandmother Duvall had died.

Grandmother Duvall was eighty-eight years old when her physical body gave way to eternity. She was strong and enjoyed good health for many years, until colon cancer invaded her liver. The day she died, I told Keli, then four years old, that her great-grandmother Duvall had gone to live with God in heaven and that she would no longer come home to live with our family. I reassured Keli in several ways that God would take care of her great-grandmother in heaven.

I'll never forget Keli's response. In fact, it impacted me so much that I wrote what she said on a small piece of paper on May 23, 1988, folded it up, and carried it with me in my wallet for nearly twenty-five years. Eventually, the old piece of paper became so tattered and torn that I decided to piece it back together with tape and store it in a very special place in my bedroom nightstand drawer.

Keli looked at me with those darling, beautiful four-year-old hazel eyes, as she prayed a prayer for her great-grandmother Duvall: "God, I hope you will help Grandmother Duvall and make her well in heaven."

These words of grace uttered by a four-year-old little girl came flooding into my consciousness twenty-five years later as I shared them with Jenna, as her brother lay dying in a hospital trauma unit.

Once again, I leaned over and touched Barrett and then softly prayed, "God, please help Barrett and make him well in heaven."

Meditation

At some point in our life, we will all pass from this earthly realm and these mortal bodies into the mystery of eternity. Some people simply lie down at night and never wake up in the morning. Sickness and/or sudden trauma claim the lives of other people. But we must never forget the hope we have in Jesus Christ as Christians, because regardless of our human circumstances, *"neither death, nor life, nor angels, nor principalities, nor powers, nor things present, nor things to come, nor height, nor depth, nor any other creature, shall be able to separate us from the love of God, which is in Christ Jesus our Lord"* (Romans 8:38-39 KJV).

CHAPTER 12

BARRETT'S FUNERAL

He heals the brokenhearted and binds up their wounds. (Psalm 147:3 NIV)

Barrett's life was full of adventure. He was so alive with energy and life prior to his death. He loved to hike and climb mountains. He even took up the challenge to ride one hundred miles with his cycling friends on a single-speed bike, no gears to shift. Now that's laughably impressive.

In recent years, he and his pastor were roommates on a mission trip to Honduras. Barrett was an incredibly gifted young man, who was a blend of an "engineer and an artist," as he was eulogized.

His pastor told the audience that while on their mission trip, Barrett touched every piece of lumber, as he helped direct the building of a home in Honduras. The pastor also shared the story of Barrett pouring himself into building a playground—a park for children in Honduras. He laughed as he shared how Barrett built a "fireman's pole" for the children and that Barrett was "the first big kid" to slide down the pole to demonstrate how it worked. He also built a swinging bridge and, of course, was the first person to cross it.

As he continued to share, the pastor said what impressed him the most about Barrett, while on their mission trip, was how he loved the children and playing with them, and then the meticulous detail Barrett provided as he helped build a home for the poor.

Robert Barrett Wood was only thirty-three years old when he died on December 3, 2012. While life is often measured by longevity, perhaps a greater measure of a person's life is the measure of its depth. Judging from Barrett's energetic engagement in life, his numerous friends, his playful heart, and loving spirit, Barrett's life had great depth.

In the days that followed Barrett's death, I had to come to grips with my own emotional vulnerability. I was still in the process of healing. I was physically and emotionally drained from the trauma my body experienced just two months earlier. I became very irritable. I prayed much, but I still had difficulty keeping my emotional equilibrium. My recovery and the death of Barrett stirred up a deep sense of my own vulnerability, and no matter how hard I tried, I lost patience with my family.

If you suffer additional trauma during your recuperation, it is important that you acknowledge your trauma, experience grief, and even seek counseling if needed. But use extreme caution that you not pick up someone else's grief. Empathize, but realize you must take care of yourself emotionally for the sake of your own recovery during your journey toward healing.

Meditation

Sit in silence. Be gentle with yourself. Let the problems of the world melt away. Pray that God will calm your spirit as you focus on slowly inhaling God's breath of life and slowly exhaling the stress and tension that threaten your emotional equilibrium.

Chapter 13

Losing Mom

O death, where is thy sting? O grave, where is thy victory? (I Corinthians 15:55 KJV)

The evening prior to Mom's passing, I was sitting on her hospital bed, holding her hand during a very intimate moment. It was amazing how lucid and alert she was, even during the waning moments of her life, as she struggled for every breath she breathed. Nevertheless, mom wanted the TV on so she could watch a football game. It didn't matter who was playing. She just wanted to watch football—not baseball—football. She made this unquestionably clear.

This was the picture of a woman who was at peace. She didn't fear death. She had rather watch football than allow death to distract her. Mom was probably wondering how much longer it was going to take for the heavenly angels to finish preparations for her arrival in heaven and was simply waiting for God to send His angels to escort her to her new home.

Still, these were my mother's final hours, and they were difficult for those of us who had to let go and entrust her soul and eternal care to God, who would heal her and give her new life in heaven.

We never forget the last words spoken to us when a loved one is slipping into eternity. Mom looked at me during those precious moments as she studied my face and said, "I like your hair." Oh, how I laughed. Then I said, "I like my hair too, mom, because I have a lot of hair, and a whole lot of guys my age don't (like, Billy Orton, a close family friend)." Mom's eyes twinkled, and she smiled. Yes, I know, for all of you guys who are bald or your hair is thinning, your comeback is, "God made only a few perfect heads, and the rest he covered with hair." Okay. Whatever.

Of course, included in Mom's last words to me, besides "I like your hair," were the words "I love you." They were words she had spoken numerous times during her final hours of life to all her children, grandchildren, and great-grandchildren. One by one, in our own individual way, all the children, grandchildren and loved ones touched "Mama Ruth," hugged her, kissed her, and expressed their love for her during the final hours of her life.

Mom's love was not only evident in her words, but more important also in her deeds. She was always there for me during the most important events in my life. Perhaps the most important life event for me was when Mom decided to show up for my birth, lest I wouldn't be here today.

The truth is my birth was more special to her than any of her other children's births, and I have flaunted in my siblings' faces many times. Of course, I have paid a price for this from Mom's other self-proclaimed favorite children, especially her favorite daughter, Tammy. If Mom were present in body, as she is in spirit, she would look at me with a disapproving look and a little quirky smile for making this statement, while glaring at me to make sure her other children knew that she loved me no more and no less than she loved all her children. But since I'm telling the story, I'll continue with my version of truth.

I was born on my mother's birthday, one minute before midnight, on September 26, 1956, and my brothers and sister can't top that! This makes me *special*.

Journey to Healing & Cherry Popsicles Too

Mom used to say, "Kyle was my greatest birthday gift but *biggest* pain." Then she would say to me, "I have always thought the doctor rolled back your time of birth a few minutes, so we could share birthdays." Mom and I celebrated those birthdays together for fifty-seven years of my life.

My mother and I will no longer have the opportunity to share our birthdays together on this earth; but while I will immensely miss these very special occasions of celebration, we will still celebrate our birthdays on September 26, every year for the rest of my life—Mom in the eternal loving presence of almighty God in heaven and me, as I continue to live out God's will and purpose for my life in these present moments.

I find myself living in two worlds. One is a temporal world; and the other world is still to come. While I live in the here and now, my hope is fixed on the eternal realm of resurrected life in communion and fellowship with the King of Kings and Lord of Lords, where my mother and father dwell today.

As Mother began to slowly drift into merciful sleep during the late evening hours of those final moments, I felt transported to the threshold of eternity. I humbly peered into the presence of God, as my mother began to draw her remaining breaths on this earth. I could only see dimly through the foggy shadows of death. I experienced grief and gratitude, as the flip sides of the same coin, during those sacred moments. What a paradox.

Foggy and dim as it was peering through those shadows, I had hope, much joy, and gratitude as I envisioned the hand of God reaching out for my mother to take her to her eternal home. *"O death, where is thy sting? O grave, where is thy victory?"* (I Corinthians 15:55 KJV).

The splendor of eternal life began to unfold in my presence, and I was reminded again, like the seven-year-old child I was when Christ entered my heart, that this same Christ of Calvary, who paid the debt for my sins, was now reaching out to my mother through resurrected love to take her safely home to dwell in the house of the Lord forever.

As a musician, I have the gift of hearing music, internally, in all of its melodies, harmonic tones, and resounding glory. During the first few days after my mother's death, as I wrestled with restless sleep, two melodic and harmonious voices comforted me during a dream state. Those voices were the presence of my mother and father. My mother and father were singing a duet that I recalled them singing when I was a child and teenager, as they proclaimed their witness for Jesus Christ in song, during Sunday morning services as the church met for worship.

As I lay ever so still, I could hear my mother and father singing these words:

"In Loving-Kindness Jesus Came"
Words: Charles H. Gabriel, 1905

In loving-kindness Jesus came
My soul in mercy to reclaim,
And from the depths of sin and shame
Thro' grace he lifted me.

From sinking sand He lifted me,
With tender hand He lifted me,
From shades of night to plains of light,
O praise His name, He lifted me!

He called me long before I heard,
Before my sinful heart was stirred,
But when I took Him at His word,
Forgiv'n, He lifted me.

His brow was pierced with many a thorn,
His hands by cruel nails were torn,
When from my guilt and grief, forlorn,
In love He lifted me.

Now on a higher plane I dwell,
And with my soul I know 'tis well;
Yet how or why I cannot tell
He should have lifted me.

From sinking sand He lifted me,
With tender hand He lifted me,
From shades of night to plains of light,
O praise His name, He lifted me!

Copyright: Public Domain
Review and Herald Publishing Association,
The Gospel in Song, 1926

And then, I slept.

So it was on September 10, 2014, my mother was reunited with my father in the glorious presence of their Lord and Savior, Jesus Christ. What a blessing. What a grace gift.

I had the honor of speaking at my mother's funeral from the very pulpit my father had led the congregation in worship. I shared the following story of hope that I once heard my father tell, as he stood in the same pulpit where I stood the day our family celebrated my mother's life—her new life in her heavenly home.

Two strangers, a small boy and an older man, were fishing from the banks of the Mississippi. As time passed, they discovered that although the fishing was rather poor, conversation was good. And by the time the sun began to sink in the west, they had talked of many things.

At dusk, a large riverboat was seen moving slowly in the distance. When the boy saw the boat, he began to shout and wave his arms that he might attract the attention of those on board. The man watched for some time and then said, "Son, you're foolish if you think that boat is going to stop for you. It's on its way to some unknown place, and it surely won't stop for a small boy."

But suddenly, the boat began to slow down, and then it moved toward the riverbank. To the man's amazement, the boat came near enough to the shore that a gangplank was lowered. The boy entered the boat, turned to his new friend on shore, and said, "Mister, I'm not foolish. You see, my father is captain of this boat, and we're going to a new home up the river."

The Captain of the riverboat arrived on the banks of eternal life on September 10, 2014, at 4:31 AM, to take Ethel Ruth Duvall, my mother, to her new eternal home up the river. She didn't have to shout or wave her arms to get the Captain's attention. Our heavenly Father knew precisely where my mother was at the moment she crossed that threshold of earthly life into eternity. God was there for my mother in the mist and fog to walk with her through *"the valley of the shadow of death."*

You see, "Mama Ruth" knew that God is faithful and His great love, mercy, and grace would never leave her or forsake her. She knew that God's eternal love, like a lighthouse beacon, would faithfully guide her to her new eternal home "up the river" at the very moment her earthly life ended.

"Death is not extinguishing the light; it is turning down the wick to trim the light for the dawn has broken" (Anonymous).

Meditation

Pray with gratitude in your heart for God's great faithfulness, love, mercy, and grace in your life and in the lives of your loved ones who have passed into eternity. Give thanks for the loved ones whose lives contributed to shaping you into the person you are today. Finally, thank God that He will never leave *you* or forsake *you*.

Chapter 14

Experiencing Grief

A fierce windstorm arose, and the waves were breaking over the boat, so that the boat was already being swamped. But He was in the stern, sleeping on the cushion. So they woke Him up and said to Him, "Teacher! Don't You care that we're going to die?" He got up, rebuked the wind, and said to the sea, "Silence! Be still!" (Mark 4:37-39 HCSB)

During the two years of my convalescence, God had immensely blessed me with physical healing in the midst of some very trying circumstances. Yet when my mother died on September 10, 2014, I was not prepared for the grief I would experience. The clouds of death and storm of loss were tossing me about like a boat lost at sea with the raging waves of grief pounding on my spirit.

Even though I had much experience in pastoral care in serving churches and had experienced the grief of losing my father prior to my mother's death, the grief I experienced in losing my mother was far different from the grief I had experienced in losing family members and loved ones in the past.

I did not sleep well for several weeks after my mother's death, and I experienced intense nightmares. I was so overwhelmed with grief that I realized it was important for me to take time off from work to focus solely on my own "grief homework" with the guidance of a professional counselor.

It were as if God stood up in the midst of my grief and directly said to me, "Silence! Be Still!" I paid attention! I literally had to be still and sit with my grief to pay attention to it, so the waves and storm of grief that were tossing me about would subside in my life.

I am blessed to know Dr. Ken Corr, congregational care minister at Brentwood Baptist Church in Brentwood, Tennessee. He provided a safe environment for me to share my nightmares, as well as the wonderful memories of my mother. He also guided me through a process of experiencing, acknowledging, and embracing my grief. The time I spent in sessions with Dr. Corr allowed me to slow down my pace and stop trying to rush through my grief. I am eternally grateful to Dr. Corr for his concern and guidance during a very traumatic time in my life.

I am also grateful that I have the privilege of working with Mr. Daryl Murray, founder and executive director of Welcome Home Ministries, in Nashville, whose spiritual depth, wisdom, and personal support provided me the necessary time off from work to help facilitate my healing. God used both Dr. Corr and Mr. Murray as lifelines of support for me during a time of great need in my life.

You may need to reach out for help, as I certainly did. You don't have to walk your journey alone. Find the professional support you need and do your "grief homework" for the sake of your own healing and eventual return to wholeness.

Saying "Goodbye" To Nancy

As I was navigating my way back to shore and the safety of solid ground, paying attention to my grief following my mother's death, little did I know at the time that death would claim the life of another family member, soon after my mother's death.

Less than two months after my mother's death, Nancy Louise Sellars, my wife's sister, died. Nancy was like a second mother to Emily; she was only sixty-six-years-old when she died, as a result of multiple physical problems.

Just two and a half weeks after Nancy was laid to rest, I awoke on Thanksgiving morning, approximately two years after I survived my own wrestling match with death. I was overwhelmed emotionally.

My mother's death had exposed every nerve ending I had, and the experience of Nancy's death was trampling on what I thought was my last nerve. Nevertheless, I wanted to speak into the lives of others in need of healing and wholeness from my own vulnerability and brokenness to share God's presence in my life in the midst of grief.

I turned to Facebook and posted the following words for my friends on Thanksgiving Day in 2014; and I e-mailed my thoughts to the senior staff and board of trustees of Welcome Home Ministries, where I work with men who desperately seek recovery from alcohol and drug addictions.

A Thanksgiving Meditation
A Difficult Thanksgiving Filled with God's Loving Presence

The emotional challenges of the past couple of months awakened me well before dawn this

Experiencing Grief

morning. Heartache and troubles have a way of invading our lives, which threaten to blind us from seeing the blessings God has so richly bestowed upon us. Sometimes it takes great effort to look beyond our myopic circumstances and lift up our eyes to gaze at the horizon of hope that lies in the distance beyond our present circumstances of hurt and pain. No one who has ever experienced great love is exempt from grief, when we are physically separated by death from the ones we so dearly love.

Yet as I wrestled in the darkness before dawn with emotions that I could not ignore (neither should you, during the times you experience grief), I find myself living a paradox—smiles through tears—as I contemplate these past two months with the reality that I have suffered great loss in the death of my dear mother, "Mama Ruth" Duvall, and, then less than two months later, my wife lost her sister, Nancy Louise Sellars.

My faith in Jesus Christ provides an opportunity for me (for all of us) to approach the very throne of God through prayer to share sorrows and joys alike.

Grief is not always experienced and expressed through tears of sadness; it is also experienced in the joyful moments of recalling and missing the presence of a dear loved one who has shaped and molded our lives through their tender loving care.

As I prayed, the cold darkness of the night and the heaviness of my heart melted away at the dawning of the sunrise of God's grace. My heart, my spirit, my soul awakened to Thanksgiving! Today, indeed, is Thanksgiving! *"This is the day the Lord has made; let us rejoice and be glad in it" (Psalm 118:24 HCSB).*

Whoever you are. Wherever you are. Whatever you have experienced that troubles you, God is with you this day of days that we call Thanksgiving.

I was blessed to have nearly fifty-eight years of life with my dear mother, who was eighty-five years old when she died. I was blessed to know Nancy Sellars for more than thirty-five years. I *am* blessed to have a wonderful wife, Emily, two children, Kyle and Keli, four grandchildren (triplets + one), brothers, a sister, and on and on and on the list goes.

As I continued to count my blessings, I was very much aware of a great truth I shared with a friend who lost a loved one. I recall saying, "Acknowledge your grief. Give grief a room in your house to live, because it is a part of you;

but don't forget that joy lives in your house too. Sometimes we must say to our grief, "Grief, I've spent enough time with you today; we will visit again. But joy lives here too, and I need to spend some time with joy."

Thanksgiving gives us an opportunity to pause and give thanks to God, even during the healing process of grief. Celebrate Thanksgiving today with a joyful heart overflowing with gratitude for God's bountiful blessings in *your* life.

How grateful I am to God for my dear family and friends and that He chose to breathe His breath of life into my being this morning to awaken me on this day of Thanksgiving.

Happy Thanksgiving!

Kyle

Chapter 15

The Glare of Death

Your heart must not be troubled. Believe in God; believe also in me. In my father's house are many dwelling places; if not, I would have told you. I am going away to prepare a place for you. If I go away and prepare a place for you, I will come back and receive you to Myself, so that where I am you may be also. (John 14:1-4 HCSB)

I sat on the front row of The Church at Station Hill, near my home in Spring Hill, Tennessee, and I read this scripture on the screen. In reading this passage, I was suddenly struck with the fact that death has glared at me and my family for much of my life—death took my grandmothers and grandfathers; cancer took my son to the very brink of death; a tragic motorcycle accident claimed the life of a dearly loved family member; I experienced the death of my father and, while I was writing this book, the deaths of my dear mother, my wife's sister, and my sister-in-law's brother.

As I sat and prayed during worship, my own experience in fighting for my life came rushing back to my awareness. I thought to myself, "How exhausting!" All the experiences of fighting to save my son's life, losing loved ones, and struggling to survive a trauma that nearly ended my earthly life were tremendously exhausting.

Nevertheless, in those moments of worship, I began to smile, as God's wondrous breath of life filled me with His presence; because while death glares at me (and at all of us at some point in life), my soul could hear the voice of Jesus saying, *"Your heart must not be troubled. Believe in God; believe also in me. . . . If I go away to prepare a place for you, I will come back and receive you to Myself"* (John 14:1-4 HCSB).

When death glares at you, don't ignore it; understand it by embracing and living life in Jesus Christ, who has conquered sin, death, and the grave and one day will come back and receive you to Himself.

The Glare of Death

The crescendo in my heart began to swell as I stood from my place of contemplative prayer to sing with other believers at the top of my lungs the following song of victory, hope, and eternal life in Christ.

Meditation
"In Christ Alone"
Lyrics: Keith Getty and Stuart Townend

In Christ alone my hope is found;
He is my light, my strength, my song;
This corner stone, this solid ground,
Firm through the fiercest drought and storm.
What heights of love, what depths of peace,
When fears are stilled, when strivings cease!
My comforter, my all in all –
Here in the love of Christ I stand.

In Christ alone, Who took on flesh,
Fullness of God in helpless babe!
This gift of love and righteousness,
Scorned by the ones He came to save.
Till on that cross as Jesus died,
The wrath of God was satisfied;
For every sin on Him was laid –
Here in the death of Christ I live.

There in the ground His body lay,
Light of the world by darkness slain;
Then bursting forth in glorious day,
Up from the grave He rose again!
And as He stands in victory,
Sin's curse has lost its grip on me;
For I am His and He is mine –
Bought with the precious blood of Christ.

No guilt in life, no fear in death –
This is the pow'r of Christ in me;
From life's first cry to final breath,
Jesus commands my destiny.
No pow'r of hell, no scheme of man,
Can ever pluck me from His hand;
Till He returns or calls me home –
Here in the pow'r of Christ I'll stand.

Copyright © 2002 Thankyou Music (PRS) (adm. worldwide
at CapitolCMGPublishing.com excluding Europe
which is adm. by Integritymusic.com)
All rights reserved. Used by permission.

Chapter 16

God's Merciful Grace

Nothing in all creation will ever be able to separate us from the love of God that is revealed in Christ Jesus our Lord. (Romans 8:39 NLT)

What do you say to parents who have watched their beloved child die from cancer or their newborn baby die at birth before it had a chance to live? What do you say to a father and mother who have lost a son in a terrible motorcycle accident, like the trauma our family experienced when Barrett's life ended in such a horrible and tragic way, just weeks before Christmas? What do you say when illness or tragedy invades and threatens *your* life, or the life of a loved one?

There are some things that only God in eternity can answer. Sometimes, it is best to say nothing at all, and pray inwardly as you sit in silence with a friend or loved one who needs your loving presence and support more than your words.

As a Christian, I find comfort in knowing that one day we who are in Christ will cross the threshold from humanity into eternity, where Jesus Christ will make us whole. Recall, again, these verses quoted earlier in this book:

> *For I am persuaded, that neither death, nor life, nor angels, nor principalities, nor powers, nor things present, nor things to come, nor height, nor depth, nor any other creature, shall be able to separate us from the love of God, which is in Christ Jesus our Lord.* (Romans 8:38-39 KJV)

It is God's merciful grace through Jesus Christ that meets us at the point of death to usher us into His eternal, loving presence. He has promised us that He will prepare a place for us and then come back for us to take us to our eternal home, where there is no suffering, sorrow, or pain.

I lived after suffering great trauma. I thank God my health has returned. I am physically whole, but had I died on that operating table, God's merciful grace would have met me at the point of my death and healed me in heaven. This is an incredible comfort for all who build their hope on the Solid Rock, Jesus Christ. Think about this for a moment, as you ponder surrendering a loved one or even your own life-threatening illness or some other trauma to God's love, mercy, and grace.

However, let me caution you during your journey toward healing and wholeness that if it is answers you seek, you may find yourself lost in a labyrinth of questions—a question behind a question ad infinitum.

It may take a while for you to move beyond the "whys" to walk in faith with hope and trust that God will take care of you or your loved ones, in life, in death, and throughout eternity. Nevertheless, my prayer is that you will surrender your life to the Lordship of Jesus Christ and experience eternal healing and wholeness found only in Jesus Christ.

As Christians, it is easy to think with the head that God will keep us in His watch-care, no matter our circumstances. But when *you* are faced with death glaring directly at you, it is your faith in Jesus Christ that will see you through the stormy gale, whether God allows you to live many more years on this earth or chooses to take you home to heal you in heaven.

When tragedy rips a loved one from our presence, especially a child, or a young mother or father dies due to an incurable illness, people often say they died "before their time."

It seems that much of our distress and argument with God is with the amount of time we are given on earth. Yet we know there are no guarantees for how long we will physically live in this world. Some die at a very old age. Some die at a young age.

Perhaps it is the death of a child or another loved one that reminds us that we too are vulnerable, we too are mortal. We human creatures need to accept our human condition and the fact that while we don't know the future, God holds our eternal future.

I have faced my mortality.

I am healthy once again.

I love life so much that I want to live forever.

I *will live* in Jesus Christ forever, as He lives in me through the power of His resurrection!

I will live in the here and now until an accident, an illness, or simply growing old claims my earthly life. It is at this point that my earthly life will transform into a spiritual awareness that I will understand only when I cross the threshold of life into the eternal, loving presence of God. Yet until then, I have a burning desire to live my life to its fullest with the hope that I may make a positive difference in the lives of people I encounter during the journey.

Yes, I grieve the loss of loved ones passed, but I rejoice that my loved ones are alive in Jesus Christ, because Jesus conquered sin, death, and the grave!

So it is that God chooses how and when to heal us. For some, it may be here on earth for yet a little while; for others, God chooses "to help them and make them well in heaven," as my little four-year-old daughter understood.

The question really is not how *long* we will live this earthly life. No one but God knows the answer to that question. The question is how *well* we will live this life by loving God, family, friends, strangers, and neighbors as we love ourselves.

The truth is, we will not have all the answers to our "whys" in this lifetime. If we had the answers to all of our "whys," we wouldn't need faith. At some point, we must put our hope and trust in something, or someone, lest we despair because we cannot solve the human condition of mortality.

If you are not building your faith and hope on the "Rock," then the shifting sand beneath your foundation will cause you to fall. Put your trust in God! Lean on Him! Build your faith and hope "on Jesus' blood and righteousness!" "All other ground is sinking sand!"

I rejoice that I have lived and continue to live this human life, because God's grace continues to breathe into me his wondrous breath of life.

I didn't become just a human being at the moment of my birth. I became a living, breathing soul! And once I cross the "Great Divide" through death into eternity, I am confidant God's merciful grace will lead me to my eternal home, where there is no more sickness, sorrow, tears, pain, or death!

God's merciful grace sustains me in life.

God's merciful grace will sustain me in death.

God's merciful grace will ultimately heal me and make me whole, and *"I will dwell in the house of the Lord forever"* (Psalm 23 KJV).

Meditation

One of the great hymns of faith that has endured throughout the ages points us in the direction of how to build hope during our journey toward healing and ultimate wholeness, when we meet God in eternity. Read the words of this great hymn, and heed them.

"The Solid Rock"
Words: Edward Mote, 1834

My hope is built on nothing less
Than Jesus' blood and righteousness;
I dare not trust the sweetest frame,
But wholly lean on Jesus' name.

On Christ the solid rock, I stand;
All other ground is sinking sand.
All other ground is sinking sand.

When darkness seems to hide His face,
I rest on His unchanging grace;
In every high and stormy gale,
My anchor holds within the veil.

His oath, His covenant, His blood
Support me in the whelming flood;
When all around my soul gives way,
He then is all my hope and stay.

When He shall come with trumpet sound,
Oh, may I then in Him be found;

Dressed in His righteousness alone,
Faultless to stand before the throne.

On Christ the solid rock, I stand;
All other ground is sinking sand.
All other Ground is sinking sand.

Copyright: Public Domain
Faith Publishing House,
Evening Light Songs, 1949, edited 1987

PARTING WORDS

As you continue your journey toward healing and wholeness, take these words with you as a beacon of hope to encourage, strengthen, and sustain you along the way:

No guilt in life, no fear in death –
This is the pow'r of Christ in me;
From life's first cry to final breath,
Jesus commands my destiny.
No pow'r of hell, no scheme of man,
Can ever pluck me from His hand;
Till He returns or calls me home –
Here in the pow'r of Christ I'll stand.

"In Christ Alone" Keith Getty and Stuart Townend, Copyright © 2002 Thankyou Music (PRS) (adm. worldwide at CapitolCMGPublishing.com excluding Europe which is adm. by Integritymusic.com)
All rights reserved. Used by permission.

The Final Chapter in Your Life Is Not Written.

Journey Onward in the Power of Jesus Christ.

To God Be All the Glory!